Professional Software

Volume I

Software Engineering Concepts

Professional Software

Volume I

Software Engineering Concepts

HENRY LEDGARD *with* JOHN TAUER

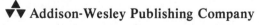 Addison-Wesley Publishing Company

Reading, Massachusetts • Menlo Park, California • Don Mills, Ontario
Wokingham, England • Amsterdam • Sydney • Singapore • Tokyo
Madrid • Bogota • Santiago • San Juan

Library of Congress Cataloging-in-Publication Data

Ledgard, Henry F., 1943—
    Professional software.

    Contents: Software engineering — Programming
practice.
    Includes bibliographies and indexes.
    1. Computer software—Development. 2. Electronic
digital computers—Programming. I. Title.
QA76.76.D47L43 1987   005   87-1760
ISBN 0-201-12231-6 (v. 1)
ISBN 0-201-12232-4 (v. 2)

ABCDEFGHIJ–AL–8987

Preface

This work treats a number of *practical* issues in software development. The issues raised here are not new but fundamental to the day-to-day concerns of the practicing professional.

In the discipline of computer science, there is a distinction to make. This is between a fundamental approach, which is necessarily quantitative, and a qualitative aspect that, while less easy to define, is equally important.

New tools, algorithms, design notations, structured editors, powerful workstations, rapid prototyping—these are exciting developments. But we must also keep sight of the more qualitative roots of our profession. These roots include:

- discipline
- teamwork
- craftsmanship
- quality

My experience suggests that, in our desire to discover new technologies, we are not always sharpening our understanding of concepts like the software development process or program readability.

Organization of This Work

The work is organized around a series of topics. Each topic relates, directly or indirectly, to the quality of software. The topics are collected into two broad categories in separate volumes.

Volume I. *Software Engineering.* This volume treats several issues that are mainly relevant to the writing of large programs. This is the area generally called *software engineering.* This includes topics such as the need to reaffirm the importance of the software lifecycle and the organization of programming teams. This section also treats the difficulties users encounter in software, an aspect of software engineering called "software human factors" or "software human engineering." Here, for example, the idea of user testing is discussed. User testing is a remarkably simple and pragmatic idea—before we ship completed systems we ought to have typical users try the system so that we can learn from their difficulties.

Volume II. *Programming Practice.* The second volume deals exclusively with programs themselves. It treats topics like the role of program comments, the persistence of global variables, and the use of packages. The underlying theme of these essays is to convey the need for careful craftsmanship in programming.

Both Volumes I and II conclude with an extended example. In developing this example, a good number of ideas mentioned in previous essays are put to practice. In Volume I, the example is developed in stages, with particular attention to the software engineering process. The final program is given as an appendix. In Volume II, the final program itself is examined. The program is presented again; this time with annotations on programming practice.

This work certainly does not address all the issues in software development. These include critical topics like planning, management techniques, resource estimating, design notations, and testing.

This book has been typeset using a monospaced font (both bold and nonbold) for programs. Monospaced typefaces, with or without bold, are most appropriate for programs. They promote readability and, I believe, give the best appearance for printing programs.

Acknowledgments

A number of people have personally influenced this work, either through my thinking about the issues or by motivating my desire to take on this effort. These include William Cave, David Gries, Jean Ichbiah, Michael Marcotty, Harlan Mills, and Andrew Singer.

Jon Hueras, over many years, has in his quiet ways continued to demonstrate the finest in software engineering.

Richard Rasala (Northeastern University), Jerry Waxman (Queens College, New York), Richard Rinewalt (University of Texas at Arlington), Charles Engelke (University of Florida in Gainesville) provided helpful review comments on an earlier version of this work. Bernhard Weinberg (Michigan State University, East Lansing), Steven Wartik (University of Virginia, Charlottesville), Richard Vidale (Boston University), and Daniel McCracken (City University of New York) thoughtfully reviewed this particular work.

The Philips courses, where I gained a clearer understanding of software quality, were under the brilliant and inspired direction of Allen Macro, assisted by John Buxton. Their book, *The Craft of Software Engineering,* is a fundamental work in the field and is based on years of experience and thinking. Nat Macon, my colleague, as well as the participants in the Philips courses, strengthened my commitment to excellence and teaching.

Howard Karger provided the photographs of the light blub and the spider web. Christine Lee provided the computer-generated piece of art depicting the cats and the graphic for program layout.

John Tauer, a professional from another discipline, assisted me on this work with his gifted pen and mind. He turned a table at Daisy's into a forum for discussing the very heart of professional practice.

H. L.

To The Reader

This book is my considered opinion about professional practice. It is derived from teaching students and professionals and from participating in numerous software efforts. The thoughtful reader may, in places, have good reason to hold other views. This should not confuse our common goal, the pursuit for excellence.

Contents

1. Programmers: The Amateur versus the Professional   1
   The Amateur   3
   The Professional   6

   SOFTWARE ENGINEERING CONCEPTS   13

2. Defending the Software Lifecycle   15
   A Miniature Lifecycle   16
   Some Important Details   19
   What Can Go Wrong   22

3. The Prototype Alternative   31
   Prototypes   32
   What Can Go Wrong   33
   Revisiting the Software Lifecycle   34

4. Programming Teams   41
   Teams—A Collective Goal   42
   Teams—An Organizational Unit   44
   Teams—Specific Tasks   47
   The Team as One's Major Activity   48
   Choosing a Team   50
   Why Teams?   52

5. The Personality Thicket   55
    Some Problems   56
    Personality   58
    Egoless Programming   61
    Can Programmers Get Better?   62

6. Work Reading and Walkthroughs   65
    Work Reading   65
    Team Walkthroughs   67

7. Misconceptions in Human Factors   71
    The Primary Goal Is to Help Novices   73
    Ease of Learning Implies Ease of Use   75
    Users Should Help Design Systems   75
    Menus Are Easier to Use Than Commands   76
    Human Engineering Centers on a Few Key Design Issues   79
    Users Will Be Comfortable with Subsets   80
    Human Engineering Is Not Particularly a Technical Matter   81
    Human Factors Are Chiefly a Matter of Taste   83
    Conclusion   84

8. Three Design Tactics from Human Factors   87
    Writing the User Manual First   88
    User Testing   90
    A Familiar Notation for Users   93

9. On Packages and Software Decomposition   101
    The Concept of a Package   103
    Packages as a Design Notation   104
    Problem Basis   106

10. Empirical Methods   111
    A Program Layout Experiment   112
    A Naming Experiment   116
    An Experiment on the Use of Procedures   117
    A Design Notation Experiment   120
    Scaling Up   121

11. What Is Successful Software?   129
    A University Project   130
    Contract Software   131
    A Commercial Product   132
    Summary   133

    SOFTWARE ENGINEERING IN MINIATURE   137

12. A Small Demonstration   139
    The Example: Text Formatting   140
    User Interface Issues   140

A Developmental User Manual   146
Specification Issues   160
Program Design   167
Program Decomposition   171
Lessons   173

Appendix: The Example Program   179

References   211

Index   215
About the Author

Contents for Volume II
Programming Practice

1. Something is Wrong, Hear

   PROFESSIONAL PROGRAMMING PRACTICE

2. One Procedure, One Purpose
   Initialization
   Gray Areas
   A Clear-cut Example

3. Developing Packages
   An Example
   Ada, Modula-2, and C

4. Global Variables
   On Mental Abstraction
   The Issues
   Own Variables and Information Hiding
   Pascal, Ada, Modula-2, and C
   Summary

5. A Note on Visibility Issues
   Name Protection
   Nested Procedures
   Nested Blocks

6. Comments: The Reader's Bridge
   Some Broad Principles
   Annotating the Obvious
   Marker Comments
   Comments with Content
   Comment Format
   Summary of Recommendations
   Pascal, Ada, Modula-2, and C

7. **The Naming Thicket**
   The Goal
   Accuracy
   Context
   Abbreviation
   Magic Constants
   Declaring Names
   Pascal, Ada, Modula-2, and C
   Escaping the Thicket

8. **Program Layout**
   Rationale
   A Lurking Principle
   Reflecting Everyday Presentation
   Comb Structures
   Layout Rules
   Summary
   C

9. **Defining Types**
   Type Name versus Variable Name
   Unnamed Types
   Enumerated Types
   C

10. **A View of Structured Programming**
    What Is It?
    The Two Guarantees of Structured Programming
    The Remaining Debate

11. **It Worked Right the Third Time**
    A Fairy Tale
    What Is a Correct Program?
    Can It Be Done?
    Why Attempt It?

PUTTING IT TOGETHER

12. **Conclusion**
    The Text Formatting Example
    What's Next

    Appendix: The Annotated Program
    References
    About the Author
    Index

1

Programmers:
The Amateur versus
The Professional

At the outset, it should be understood that an endeavor to compare an amateur and a professional does not describe the full hierarchy in programming or any other vocation or avocation. The complete spectrum might be: the ignorant, the novice, the aficionado, the amateur, the professional, and the master.

Music, expressly classical music, comes to mind if all six rankings were to be defined. The novice appreciates Tchaikovsky's 1812 Overture every Fourth of July when the cannons go off along the Charles River in Boston. The novice learns the notes of the scale in order to play an instrument (the guitar, usually). The aficionado can tell the difference between Mozart and Mahler, the amateur can play the first two movements of the "Moonlight" sonata, and the professional can play all 32 Beethoven sonatas. The master writes the music that eventually finds its way into the repertoire.

The distinction between amateur and professional that we are making, however, is not a simple matter. Consider an analogy with a golfer. Given some basic talent, capable instruction, and a good deal of practice, a young player can play close to par golf and decide to pursue a career as a professional. After a perfunctory declaration or surviving the qualification tournaments, he may end up as a club pro or be invited to the Master's

Tournament. But his status is clearly defined. What he can or cannot do in golf is limited by his skill. Not so with programmers.

In the past ten years there has been a revolution in the computer industry so that a politician could rightfully campaign for a computer in every home rather than a chicken in every pot. It would be difficult to speculate on how many new computer owners are either ignorant of programming or are novices in the practice. But imagine the delight of the novice when his first program is written:

```
10 REM THIS IS AN ADDING MACHINE
20 LET A = 2
30 LET B = 3
40 LET Y = A + B
50 PRINT Y
```

The answer comes out 5 and a new programmer is born!

So this example is facetious. Perhaps our novice programmer writes a program that determines the date of Easter in any year from 1415 to 2030 and is writing a paper on Pope Pius II. Imagine the delight to find that this humanist pope did indeed celebrate Easter Mass on April 19 in 1460, as calculated by the program. Now the novice programmer is almost an amateur.

If at first the computer was a fascination for the very few, it has created a romance that is now a fiber of both industry and academia. No major corporation with even the smallest industrial base can function without a staff of programmers. There is a proliferation of computer courses in colleges and universities across the country. Programming is now even an integral part of some high school curricula. In sum, millions of people know how to program to some degree.

A generation of amateur programmers is afoot across the land. And that's all right. Many find programming useful as an addendum to a career in another field, perhaps in biology or management. Often they are good programmers who are not paid primarily for their programming skills. They may indeed be highly skilled in certain aspects of programming and even consider themselves expert programmers.

Those whom we call professionals are experienced coders, university graduates, engineers, system developers, computer scientists, or application specialists. They are paid for their computer expertise, which is their specialty. The purpose of this work is to define a professional as one who has a grasp of the quantitative requirements of this area along with an understanding of the qualitative demands that are necessary to this high calling.

Let us examine these two entities, the amateur and the professional, in their own idealized worlds.

The Amateur

The amateur can be proud—the world of the amateur is properly limited. The amateur programmer usually writes programs:

- For a limited number of users, often only for the author;
- That can crash under varied and bizarre input;
- That can result in unusual but acceptable output;
- That only the author needs to be able to read;
- That need not be fully tested;
- That require little documentation;
- Without regard to user requirements;
- Without regard to some defined software lifecycle (see Figure 1.1 for the textbook variant);
- Without regard to integration with other, larger, or future systems.

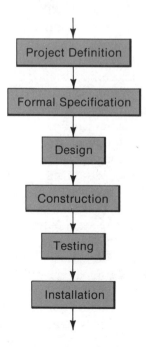

Figure 1.1   The software lifecycle

This little taxonomy is not critical, only descriptive of the amateur programmer. Think of the number of calendars our Renaissance historian would have had to count to arrive at the date of Easter in 1460. The amateur programmer may be a hobbyist who writes programs to play games or draw pictures, a scientist who writes programs to analyze data, or a university student who writes a program to fulfill a course or thesis requirement. In each case, the programs are written without a need for anyone else to understand, debug, or maintain them.

A number of issues are unimportant when programs are written for individual use. It doesn't matter if input formats are unwieldy or inconvenient or if the program doesn't work well or all of the time—as long as it works most of the time. These shortcomings are acceptable. What may seem to be bizarre and unusual input does not concern the amateur programmer. In writing a program for solving the roots of an equation, for instance, it matters little that someone might enter inputs consisting of carriage returns, people's names, or strange control codes. The amateur knows what the program is supposed to do and these unreasonable data may well be unreasonable to worry about.

Likewise, the output for the amateur need not be satisfying or pleasing in format, style, or screen layout. More often than not, the program is used only occasionally and only the programmer needs to understand the output. Consider a program designed to compute areas. If measurements are given to an accuracy of only three decimal places, the program might be written using real arithmetic and the output displayed to ten decimal places. To another user of the program this might be annoying, but it does not bother the author, who simply disregards the last seven decimals and presses forward.

For the amateur, the program itself need not be that readable. Matters like choosing appropriate names, organizing the program into simple logical units, or giving the program a well-spaced appearance are not of vital concern. Most programmers can read their own programs and fix or debug them when necessary. It's the other person's program that causes trouble.

The amateur seldom has to test a program thoroughly. The only requirement may be to achieve certain output requirements. The fact that some of the control paths have never been exercised is not of much concern in either planning or testing the program.

Programming is now widespread in most disciplines and business activities. In one form or another, it has become more critical to our daily activities. Suppose that a corporation develops a piece of software to handle a payroll. Such a program must be written in such a way to have a long life span, and eventually hundreds of people may be involved in simply keeping the program up to date with current payroll requirements.

This is a different game than the amateur plays. The amateur hardly needs to see the implications of a program, how it affects more than just one person, the programmer himself. If the program "does the job," it's all right. If there is any practice that an amateur develops, it is a kind of well-directed tunnel vision for the result: by Jove, it works! And if it works, that's it.

The amateur is not particularly concerned about documenting a program. If the program performs reasonably and the output is fairly consistent, no documentation is required because the program works. No one else has to learn the program, no one else has to maintain it.

And why would an amateur care about the lifecycle of software? The program is the programmer's alone. Any ideas about software specifications are not relevant. User requirements are not a consideration because the programmer is the only user. The requirement is met when the program works, even if the program is fairly complicated. Whatever particular (and personal) needs are required or suggested along the way, the amateur programmer can change the behavior of the program to meet these needs. Features can be added or subtracted, more or less, at will. No one else will be affected.

Any commercially necessary program, such as the payroll program mentioned earlier, has another dimension about it that need not concern the amateur: estimating the resources needed to do the job and estimating the length of time the task will take. Of course, the professor meeting a research deadline at the university has some concern for a time schedule. However, the traditional software lifecycle (see Figure 1.1), which includes planning, specification, design, construction, testing, and actual user operation of the program, is hardly relevant and probably a nuisance.

Finally, there is the matter of integrating a program into the software of a larger system. Reasonably, the amateur never considers this in the program design. Creating a generalized sorting package for use inside an operating system or writing a general-purpose formatting program are tasks beyond the concerns of the amateur programmer. These kinds of programs must interface with other programs and, in a general sort of way, with the conventions and protocols of the supporting environment. These are the kind of considerations that describe the requirements for any kind of software that is needed, the kind of host for which a program can be written.

If all this describes an idealized world of a skilled amateur programmer, it is simply a world where some quiet, personal work must be accomplished.

The Professional

Something has happened. In my view, there are many programmers who have been pushed into professional roles for which they are ill equipped or are locked into a purely quantitative practice of programming. This is a more subtle observation than it seems. Paralleling our description of the amateur, another shading might be interjected into the spectrum so that we have:

Ignorant
Novice
Aficionado
Amateur
    Amateur who thinks he is a professional
    Amateur who is learning to be a professional
    Professional who is really an amateur
    Professional who did not reach out
Professional
Master

The indented categories are not quite interchangeable, but they exist only at this level of the spectrum. For example, there are no professionals who pose as masters, just as there are few aficionados who presume to be more than intense devotees of the subject. Once again, applying this spectrum to music (and it is just as applicable to any profession), I have a middle-aged friend who is an aficionado of music, who still takes an occasional piano lesson from a professional. But he loves music for the joy of it and doesn't think of himself as an amateur—just as his mentor who holds a chair in a symphony orchestra would not presume to be a master. Both understand, respect, and enjoy their relationship with music.

It is a matter of attitude and status. If we use the symbol P to denote a professional, we could denote this new rank by the term P-sub-A—something between an amateur and a professional. Consider all four shadings:

1. The *amateur who thinks he is a professional* might be a graduate whose knowledge is enough to impress those who are unfamiliar with the profession. Such programmers think they are better than they are. The tragedy, as we shall see, is when this attitude is taken to the office.

2. We should be encouraged by the *amateur who is learning to be a professional.* It is here that we must understand that most professionals were once amateurs, that most of them passed through a transitional phase in their development. I would think that many undergraduate and

graduate students are more than amateurs, less than professionals. It's too bad that an old term has passed out of our lexicon—journeyman. It is a much more appealing description, for it implies a positive attitude and a mobile status.

3. The *professional who is really an amateur* is a reflection of status that cements an attitude. Our profession often propels some beyond their capabilities. It is inexpedient to hire new personnel when a familiar hand can be promoted. The requirements of the new post are professional, but the individual has elements of amateur ability. The new status creates (and maybe demands) a professional attitude, but the skills are not all there. Defensiveness and overconfidence set in.

4. The *professional who did not reach out* is a description of one who has not taken the time to learn or, more likely, one who succumbs to the pressures of a given situation. The problems vary, and there will always be moments that are the hallmark of a professional.

So, in some cases, we have a journeyman; in others, an immobile programmer who is likely to remain so. It does not detract, however, from the situation as I have come to understand it. We think (looking upward) that the programming world looks like Figure 1.2a, but my experience has led me to believe that it looks like Figure 1.2b. Many "professionals" are assumed professionals. The true professional is found less often than we think.

Do not take this matter lightly. It is the substance of my arguments. Let me show you why. Consider Figure 1.3, which contains some observable characteristics of programmers. You see that we are attempting to define our goal: the description of the *true* professional programmer.

In no way do I wish to suggest here that the professional's task is easy. The task may not even be under the professional's control. Consider:

The project may be so fragmented (Fred's group is doing the user interface; Janet's group, the memory management) that hope for success is dim, diminished at best.

The project may be based on a prototype that eventually overwhelms the project.

The people involved (management, peers, marketing, support) may exhibit such wide differences that creative skills are nearly impossible to harness.

Perhaps the programmer should quit. Ah, but let us not stray from our course.

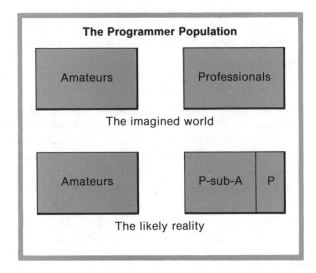

Figure 1.2   The programmer population

Professionals write programs upon which other people depend. This could be a piece of software that is commercially available—a program written for a microcomputer in a car, an orbiting satellite, or a mobile telephone unit. It could also be a program that is used to make the monthly billings or schedule courses at a university. The common characteristic of these kinds of programs is that other people make use of the software directly or indirectly. Many users are affected by the programmer's work.

When other people are involved as users, the programmer's task becomes much more difficult. Most software users do not understand the inner workings. They become confused by its operation and are apt to type all sorts of things as input into the program. In a word-processing program, if a user is unsure of how to get out of a text-editing mode, for instance, all kinds of consequences can occur. The user can type control codes, carriage returns, file names, and words like "help" or "quit." Even something apparently clear, like responding to a computer-prompted question, can lead to surprises. The professional must try to account for these spurious cases in writing a program.

Many users demand nearly perfect implementations and are generally impatient with faulty software. The first-time user of a program, especially one who was expecting a Christmas-night reward with a new "toy," may be not only impatient but discouraged: the promises of the program were

Figure 1.3
Observable Attitudes

The P-sub-A programmer:	The professional programmer:
1. Perpetuates the mythical user (assumes the user is just like the programmer).	1. Writes programs for a large class of users (does *not* assume user knowledge).
2. Lives in "systems mentality" where dealing with anomalies is a way of life.	2. Worries about "unusual" cases.
3. Considers work reading (that is offering one's own work for open criticism) as a nuisance.	3. Writes programs that *anyone* can read.
4. Keeps trashing out the bugs.	4. Releases programs with *no* known errors or strange features.
5. Deals with documentation later.	5. Writes documentation *first.*
6. Is always "programming"—always developing some new feature on the terminal.	6. Negotiates and develops the user requirements and functional specification in great detail.
7. Doesn't see the software lifecycle slowly fall apart.	7. Has well-defined phases with hard benchmarks.
8. Gets on with the job.	8. Writes programs with concern for future and larger systems.

unfulfilled. For the professional programmer, this is a concern at the inception of the program. The software requirements, team composition, attitude toward work, software tools, and schedule—all bear heavily on the ultimate reliability of the program.

An issue that the amateur almost never needs to consider, but is vital to the professional, is the matter of documentation. Documentation is the means by which other people can specify what the software is to accomplish, a job description, as it were. It is a means to describe one's work to others. There may be preliminary documents describing the intent of the system, project planning, sketches of the technical requirements, user manuals, test data specifications, training guides, and maintenance information. On most projects, these documents are not superfluous. Often they are the cornerstones for defining and measuring progress. For the amateur, a few scruffy pages may be adequate. For the professional, documentation may be the hallmark of the product.

It is a fallacy to think of documentation as neutral to software behavior. It is not, or at least should not be, an after-the-fact process. Documentation should precede implementation. Written commitments may be needed for a given feature or a given style of behavior. Protocols for the user interface may need to be established. Performance requirements on the speed or use of resources may have to be spelled out. In some cases, the better ones, a preliminary user manual is written before a line of final software is started. Even if the traditional lifecycle model (Figure 1.1) is not used (for instance, basing the project on a prototype), the documentation at least serves as a blueprint for the project.

Professional software must often be integrated with other components of a software or hardware system. A program that handles the management of files in an operating system, for example, must be integrated with the text-editing facilities. This means that the software does not stand alone. Protocols for input and output may dictate severe constraints on any supporting software. Often the programmer has no latitude in these matters, but must go to great detail to guarantee that the behavior of software is accurate.

Beyond these more or less technical requirements, there is another issue that *dramatically* distinguishes the professional from the amateur and that is: A professional does not work in isolation. Most professional software projects are simply too extensive for a single person to conceive, write, and maintain.

Projects of the professional dimension have given rise to developing software with a team of participants. Like a professional football team, the professional programming team is a collection of people who combine different skills working toward a single goal—a completed software project. Working with others involves many social and organizational aspects. In many cases, a piece of software may have to be read hundreds of times before it is publicly released. This puts a responsibility on the author of the program unit. Every minute wasted trying to understand what a particular construct means, every hour wasted wondering how a particular module works, and every day or week wasted when an error is discovered and corrected can result in more loss for the entire project.

The viability of a general programming effort can be hampered by individual idiosyncrasies. Ideas that were suppressed might be the very ones that other team members need to solve the problem at hand. Others may make bold talk of their own excellence or think that some completed sub-project is good when it is not. The professional's role is to set exceptionally high standards of behavior. This means not only understanding that all ideas are important, but also realizing that no single team member can consider his or her contribution without fault or criticism.

In some software projects, outside evaluators are called upon to make an independent assessment. This can be a general-purpose review or, later, extensive live testing. The professional welcomes these critiques. A good testing phase is rigorous and thorough. Often the process is automated, in that predefined sets of data are fed to the software. Boundary conditions, spurious input, and exceptional cases are all tried.

Professional software is often useful for a long time, typically five to ten years. Unlike buying an automobile, the maintenance issue is far more pervasive. There used to be an adage that if you got a "lemon" from Detroit, it was probably a "Monday-morning" car or was built just before new tooling was put on line. Different automobiles may have different maintenance problems, but the software maintenance problem is fundamentally different. Really, for software, "maintenance" is the wrong word.

> Unlike automobiles, software does not wear out. For given input, software continues to produce the same output.

> A sizable part of maintenance goes into altering aspects that were not well understood when the software was initially written. We may later realize that the software takes too much memory, ignores some important case, or crashes under unforeseen circumstances.

> Once the software is in use, demands for it change. Yesterday's word processor did not handle footnotes, today's must.

When software goes awry or updates are needed, the authors may have forgotten what was really in the program or may have moved on to other projects. It may be absurd to think that one can find a good mechanic for a 1933 Essex, but one should expect that bugs or updates in a 1983 payroll program can be handled by any good software engineer. Actually, one should expect that there be no bugs at all in the software.

The problem of software produced in a hurry is that maintenance is not a priority in design. Planning for maintenance becomes largely a token homage issue. When things are not quite right, the user is often stuck with a lemon but has no warranty to exercise. On the one hand, overconfident programmers *think* their software is maintainable; on the other hand, most of them complain about the "other person's" software they are assigned to maintain. Quite simply, maintainable software is seldom written.

Consider a final comparative:

Observable Attitudes

The P-sub-A programmer: *The professional programmer:*

9. Writes software for the computer.   9. Writes software for the human reader.

For the P-sub-A programmer, the human reader is an aside. For the true professional, the computer is only a necessary prerequisite. The human reader is paramount.

The world of the amateur and the professional are strikingly different. So, too, are the worlds of the assumed professional (P-sub-A) and the true professional. These differences are observable. Ultimately the differences are manifest in the *quality* of their work.

Software Engineering Concepts

2

Defending the Software Lifecycle

In the early years of programming, when Fortran was *the* language and Algol 60 a hope for the future, the software lifecycle was almost a secret. Yes, some wise few had discovered the secret but, even in the emerging centers of computer research in the 1960's, the concept was more or less unknown.

Today, the concept evokes some strong reactions. There are divergent views about the lifecycle, which are roughly represented as:

- The lifecycle is the cornerstone of development.
- The lifecycle is out of date; it doesn't work with today's rapidly changing technology.
- Get good people and the lifecycle will manage itself.
- Prototypes are the answer—not the lifecycle.
- Are there other ways to write software?

If you look at texts on software engineering, you will find frequent mention of the lifecycle, perhaps with different names or alternative versions, almost always at the beginning of the text.

If you look at what happens in practice, you might conclude that the lifecycle does not exist, that almost everyone practices it, or that almost no one practices it. Your conclusion depends on your definition. Are we playing with mirrors?

Note: In my graduate student years at MIT (1964-1969) I do not recall any mention of the concept of a "software lifecycle." My first detailed exposure to the concept was about 1973, through Bill Cave. Bill Cave has recorded his views in a book, *Software Lifecycle Management* [Cave and Maymon, 1984].

A Miniature Lifecycle

To understand the root idea behind any variant of the lifecycle, it is instructive to consider a tiny project, the writing of a utility routine or a short student project. One good example is a program to generate a random permutation of integers between 1 and some input value N. If N is 10, for example, the output might be

    8 6 3 1 5 10 2 4 7 9

A program for this problem might only be a page or two, but it is not trivial.

A familiar development scenario is the following:

> The programmer decides to write a routine to generate a sequence of random numbers between 1 and N. This may require a little research to obtain and understand the random number algorithm, but the algorithm is fine and easily coded. The routine requires the user to enter the seed for the random sequence. This routine is written and tested.
>
> Next the question of a permutation is considered. This suggests the use of an array to record random numbers already chosen. This part requires some small modifications to the code already written, but this is handled.
>
> When the program is run, the programmer decides to revise the prompting messages, the layout of the output, and the actions in case of incorrectly formed input (for example, entering H00 instead of 100). Finally, the entire program is satisfactory.

This is *not* a software lifecycle.

A different scenario might go like this:

> The programmer examines the input-output requirements. User-defined values must be entered: (a) the seed, (b) the value of N. Clear prompting messages are written, erroneous input is enumerated, and the layout of the output is determined. These decisions are written down as program header comments. The input-output specification is, at least hopefully, exact and complete. (*Specification*)
>
> The programmer examines the random number generation problem as well as the permutation issue. The random number algorithm is resolved, and the method to give permutations is understood. (*Design*)

The program itself is now written. (*Construction*)

The program is tested and any errors are repaired. No change is made to the input or output. (*Testing*)

This *is* a lifecycle. Notice, one could say that the first scenario is most appropriate in this case, since most of the effort may be problem solving. One could also say that the second scenario is too rigid.

Fundamentally, the second scenario is a lifecycle (see Figure 2.1) because

- The development process evolves in *distinct* stages.
- Each stage is *completed* before the next begins.

This is the essence of any lifecycle—distinct, complete stages. All too often the development of professional software resembles the first scenario. Little is learned about software development. While perfect lifecycles may not exist, the lifecycle idea is a *goal* or target for software development.

For professional software, the lifecycle chosen will depend on the scale and complexity of the system. For contract software, we might have a lifecycle like that in Figure 2.2. Here each phase may require several months work, and feedback to a previous stage may be a significant issue to control. But the same point applies. The more distinct and the more complete each stage is, the closer it is to the ideal. If the construction stage significantly affects the approved design, there is a problem. If installation significantly affects the user requirements, there is a more critical problem.

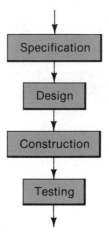

Figure 2.1   A miniature lifecycle

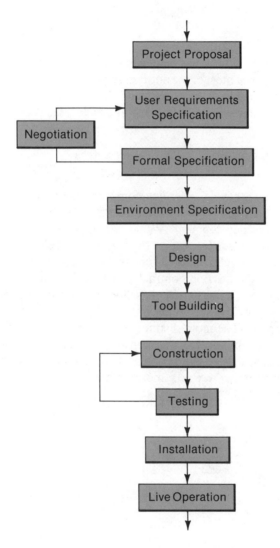

Figure 2.2   One possible lifecycle for contracted software

In essence, then, a software lifecycle is a sequence of stages for producing software. Software production, instead of a continuing process of parallel, undiscriminated activities as we see during the first scenario, is broken down into distinct stages. Each stage has a definite beginning and a definite ending. Each stage treats a specific, defined set of issues. Thus one stage sets the groundwork for the next stage, but the activities of each are fundamentally different. The process proceeds on a footing where both organizational and technical issues are considered at relevant points.

Some Important Details

Let us consider the lifecycle of Figure 2.3 and some of its characteristics, as listed in Figure 2.4. I call this the textbook lifecycle, for it is kind of a common denominator, suggestive of textbooks on the subject. It contains the rudiments of many (but not all) lifecycles.

The textbook software lifecycle has six discrete stages. In the first stage, *Project Definition,* the emphasis is on outlining the proposed project, defining the resources needed for the project, negotiating with the user or customer, and, generally, making a definite project plan. The result of the project definition stage is a written document describing the project as a whole and accompanied by a User Requirement Specification or, for short, a URS. This is a statement of the project as seen by the user. If the project is justified, the documents are signed and approved.

The next stage, *Formal Specification,* is more technical in nature. Here the exact specifications of the project are identified, the behavior of the system (as seen by the user) is defined in detail, and the protocols are established for the rest of the project. A major output of this stage is a "Functional Specification," a technical description of the entire project. This is also where user documentation should be written. One ideal output from this phase is a preliminary user's guide or a user's reference manual. One might think of the functional specification and the user manual as similar to architectural drawings for the design of a building. Detailed and technical, they describe the exact nature of the system. The documents, of course, should be signed and approved before further development proceeds.

In the *Design* phase, critical data structures and algorithms are developed and the general structure of the software is refined. Prototypes may be built. Experiments may be run to test different strategies for the human interface. User testing, the testing of trial software with representative users, should be performed to test the viability of design ideas.

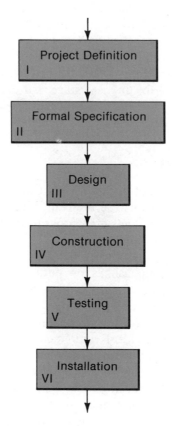

Figure 2.3   The textbook software lifecycle

The next stage, *Construction,* is where programming the final product begins. This stage is the beginning of top-down coding and top-down integration of modules. In this stage, specific coding conventions and other development standards are adopted and put in place. The required hardware, which should be available before this stage, is used. The output of this stage should be a complete working system.

The *Testing* stage involves a full-scale use of the program in a live environment. It is here that the software and hardware are shaken down, anomalies of behavior are eliminated, and the documentation is updated to reflect final behavior. The testing must be as thorough as possible. The use of adversary roles at this stage is an extremely valuable tool because it ensures that the system works in as many circumstances as possible.

Figure 2.4
Some Typical Characteristics of a Lifecycle

I. *Project Definition*

1. Frequent user contacts
2. Elimination of arbitrary constraints
3. Scaling down of features
4. Hard negotiations
5. Statement of assumptions
6. Project plan and estimates
7. Signed go-ahead

II. *Formal Specification*

1. Complete technical specification
2. Preparation of preliminary user manual
3. Detailed project plan
4. Specification of needed resources (equipment, software)
5. Signed approval of user manual and technical specification

III. *Design*

1. Resolution of critical problems
2. Design of critical data structures and algorithms
3. Trial implementations and prototypes
4. User testing
5. Go, No-go review

IV. *Construction*

1. Adoption of standard coding conventions
2. Top-down development and integration
3. Schedule of module development
4. Preparation of Test Sets
5. Complete Module Test

V. *Testing*

1. Full-scale use in life-like environment
2. Shake-down of user documentation
3. Adoption of formal change procedures
4. Signed release

VI. *Installation*

1. Procedures for handling errors and changes
2. Adoption of change control plan
3. Periodic reviews with the user

The last stage in the software lifecycle is *Installation*. Here the system is installed in a customer environment or put in the catalogue for sale. In this stage, there should be procedures for getting some kind of user feedback on the true usability of the system, its speed of execution, the amount of storage, and so on. Periodically, there should be reviews with users or customers to determine to what degree the system actually meets expectations.

Note: Other thoughtful views of the lifecycle models are given in [Fairley, 1985] and [Marco and Buxton, 1987].

What Can Go Wrong

Sometimes we are better served by example than by pronouncement. The imagined letter at the end of this chapter has in it my arguments for the software lifecycle. If, in reality, it has not been written, it might have been— to numerous software engineering project managers. This is a diversion, but only in style—not in substance. This letter sketches some broad observations about a project in difficulty; what happens as the "theory" falls apart.

To visualize this, consider Figure 2.5. It typifies the kind of feedback among the stages of a lifecycle. Such feedback is normal, but not all of it may be favorable. Some feedback always occurs. Writing software is an intrinsically human process. An unnoticed problem spotted during construction may call for a change in design. The ideal is to keep the feedback to a minimum. The goal of the front-end loading, inherent in a well-kept lifecycle, is to anticipate problems. A problem resolved in advance is not a problem.

Next consider Figure 2.6, which depicts overlapping in the stages of a lifecycle. This sequence is also counter to the essence of any lifecycle. I do not mean that elements in a later stage are never present earlier. A design issue may need to be resolved before a specification issue is put to rest. Code may be written to test performance issues in a design. But this "peeking" into later stages is done to resolve the *current* stage.

One line of attack to preserve the lifecycle is the isolation of clear benchmarks. Consider the following list of benchmarks.

The user requirement specification is completed.
The documentation plan is written.
The user goals have been written down.
The preliminary user manual is completed.
The coding standards have been written.
All the code has been compiled.
The code has passed an external quality review.

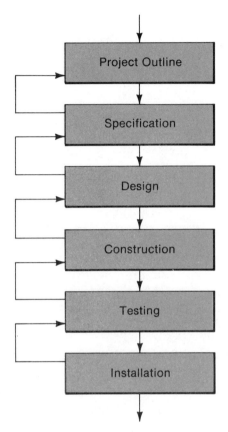

Figure 2.5   Feedback in a software lifecycle

What about these? Well, some are fine, some illusory.

The user requirement specification is completed. This is an excellent early benchmark.

The documentation plan is written. The key to this is "written." Simply being written is one matter—being approved is another.

The user goals have been written down. This probably means a list of platitudes. How serious are the user's concerns? How will the goals be tested to see if they have been achieved? Tests that measure how well the user goals have been satisfied is much better. If the tests have been approved, even better.

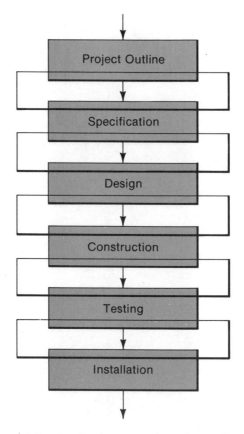

Figure 2.6   Overlap in stages of a software lifecycle

The preliminary user manual is completed. Fine, but only if completed means truly finished (i.e., edited, reviewed, complete with examples and with appendices). Completing the preliminary user manual is a worthy milestone. Of course, having it approved is even better.

The coding standards have been written. This is an uncertain benchmark. Programmers may reject the standards. The standards may be too confining or too lax. But a benchmark that includes consent by members of the project team will be a positive step.

All the code has been compiled. Nice, but doesn't mean much. The code may be a disaster or it may be an elegant piece of work. The simple fact that it is written is of no interest or value.

The code has passed an external quality review. Bingo! A benchmark for a true professional.

Carving solid benchmarks is seldom easy. When development proceeds without marked stages, the vision necessary to monitor and control progress is often blurred.

The diagrams of Figures 2.5 and 2.6 lead to a combined form, Figure 2.7. Here the lifecycle has effectively disintegrated, an invitation to disaster.

No matter what the development process, some projects get finished and the product is released. A software lifecycle offers a chance for control, for learning, for quality. Project plans mean something; benchmarks are meaningful. When the software development process is directed, the chances for success are more than improved.

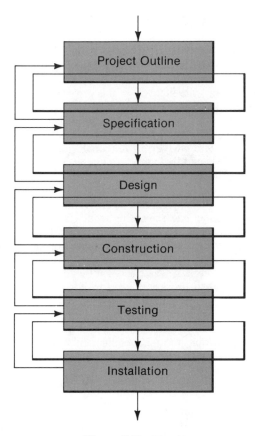

Figure 2.7   Trouble

COMPUTER AUDITS, LTD.

Highrise Building   •   *New York, New York*   •   10023

July 14, 1986

William B. Smythe, Program Manager
DeltaSoft Products, Inc.
11 Technology Circle
Boston, MA 02114

Dear Bill:

SUBJECT: PRELIMINARY AUDIT—PROJECT SPREAD-CALC

This cover letter gives my observations, conclusions, and recommendations from our recent audit of the Spread-Calc Project being developed at DeltaSoft Products. This audit was conducted during the month of June, 1986. At your request, special attention was paid to the software lifecycle of this project. Detailed documents from the audit will follow within a week.

In the past three years, COMPUTER AUDITS has examined various development projects, one-of-a-kind systems, and new product efforts—all with the purpose of examining software lifecycles. Our conclusion, in many instances, is the idea of a software lifecycle generally fades during project development until virtually nothing particularly visible remains.

This report to you, then, is also a summary of other visits and, as such, may appear as too many generalizations where specifics are sought. But we at COMPUTER AUDITS have had rewarding feedbacks from this kind of critique because names and events are not necessary when a critical examination of a method is made. We hope that you share this report of audit with your staff, especially your senior programmers.

After a month's observation, it was clear that the idea of a software lifecycle at DeltaSoft had little more than lip service paid to it. Specifically, as concerns the Spread-Calc project:

1. The project plan was rather evasive.
2. Little resembling a written, formal specification was found.
3. Programming occurred throughout the project.
4. Visible benchmarks were hard to find.
5. The user documentation came after the majority of the code had been written.
6. Updates were planned before the final release.
7. The software was released with known anomalies of behavior.

Page 2
July 14, 1986

The general impression I received from most of your programmers was that these were not indications of amateur attitudes or procedures; on the contrary, they seemed to feel that great things were happening with Spread-Calc.

Your group worked diligently for many months, with much overtime. This itself should tell you that all was not well beforehand.

The substance of this audit is that DeltaSoft should institute measures incorporating a software lifecycle before another project is begun. I submit to you, Bill, that the software lifecycle is the cornerstone of professional practice. With that in mind, I think it's necessary for you folks at DeltaSoft to be alert to some aspects that have caused the idea of the software lifecycle to lapse.

1. Project Plan

An early weakness in reviewing and auditing Spread-Calc was the project plan. We were unable to find a project timetable as such that was completed during the project, that gave dates on which the items were due, or that generally described the sequence of activities on the project. A project plan can simply be a few pages or (in larger projects) a small book. The project plan must have the flexibility to be revised during the project so that it is kept up to date. Its goal is control. It makes the project visible through explicit plans that are taken seriously.

Too often, a project plan is merely a throw-away document meant to satisfy project management. The project plan must serve the project itself; and, in the long run, is used for learning about the general management of software. Ideally, one might review the project plan of a past project before writing the next one for a new project.

One of the cornerstones of a good project plan is explicit benchmarks. These are items of work that must be completed during the lifetime of the project and should be signed off by those responsible when they are completed. Benchmarks are visible and they are "hard," not to be bypassed even when pressure for project completion increases.

This is not to say, Bill, that all software lifecycles are the same. For smaller projects, the idea of the software lifecycle need not—should not—be abandoned. The activities performed within each stage of a lifecycle will be different. But the point will always be the same: the product is developed in discrete stages with definite outputs and definite benchmarks associated with each stage. Definite benchmarks are glaringly absent in our audit of Spread-Calc.

2. Formal Specification

When you first called me suggesting an audit, you made the remark that you were surprised how the Spread-Calc project was getting out of hand. This problem, as we both noticed from the outset, began at the specification stage (what there was of it). Your top programmers are no different from all the others we have seen—they are an ambitious lot who tackle anything. The result of this is that the project requirements

Page 3
July 14, 1986

tended to escalate. As we both know, quality work requires additional effort. Unknowingly, the norm becomes a sacrifice of quality for quantity.

Spread-Calc is a classical example of the constant pressure organizations like DeltaSoft get for more elaborate projects—projects that, I need not remind you, are intrinsically expensive. You are finding hidden overhead costs, maintenance costs, and how one project can drag the whole organization. When matters get out of hand, as they slowly did with Spread-Calc, we found that responsibility was spread out among more and more interested parties—the result was that Spread-Calc became more complex and more ambitious than it was intended to be. Your problem, then? "Too many cooks spoiled your broth." This need not have happened if a functional specification had been the focus for development.

Your programmers, like most, suffer from what I call "feature syndrome." Spread-Calc has some unique features: good recovery in case of user error, good cursor movement, and an excellent query facility, to mention a few. But by failing to consider the formal specification seriously, Spread-Calc did not have a good user design. By that, regardless of the "features," you have to look at the "whole:" consistent interpretation, a pleasant user interface, an appealing screen, a smallness of scale, and a consistency across separate subsystems.

I was not on board for the negotiations, but I think it will be helpful to you to think back. One of the first goals in development is to negotiate the project itself. One should go for a *minimum* set of sound features needed to do the job well. Were the users asking for or were you suggesting too many features for Spread-Calc? The questions you should have addressed at that time were:

What is the true functionality of the system (rather than a perceived functionality)?

What scale is reasonable, whether on-line help was reasonable to add (it was botched and should have been skipped)?

What quality aspects are needed?

None of these issues is easy, but they have a great effect on the ultimate success of the project.

The sum of these remarks is that you need not be reluctant to attempt ambitious projects like Spread-Calc or plan for even more powerful systems. But the larger the scope, the more you must be aware of what the user really needs. This is captured technically in a functional specification.

My opinion about Spread-Calc is that it is a project that just happened. It seems to have evolved from many, spurious sources which grew to achieve a life of their own; and, somehow or other, achieved a final state of implementation. If you haven't come to grief over Spread-Calc yet, I think you will. It may be the right time (and it may save you a great deal of money) to start thinking about Spread-Calc II employing a software lifecycle that will turn the project around.

Page 4
July 14, 1986

    I am enclosing a little card that I found on the desk of a programmer whom I admire, one of the few I have seen using the software lifecycle I have outlined in this critique. See what it implies? It means doing more, much more, before final coding. Coding is done near the end of the project, after other aspects have been resolved. It is in this sense that the software lifecycle is about "front-end loading." It is as if one is always preparing for the future.
    I hope this preliminary letter will be of help to you.

Yours in better programming,

Sam Weber

Sam Weber
Chief, Audit Division

Enc.   A notecard

FRONT-END LOADING

☑ Plan, before doing
☑ Negotiate the requirements
☑ Document first
☑ Prepare a complete specification
☑ Design before coding
☑ Commit resources on time
☑ Build prototype or facade
☑ Do user testing early

3

The Prototype Alternative

With the pressures of a competitive marketplace, the lifecycle model itself has been questioned. Criticism takes various forms:

- Too much planning
- Too slow
- Too much waste
- Inability to adapt to change
- Failure to accommodate developing technology

One of the purposes of extensive planning and preparation of the lifecycle is to minimize change. But changes do and must take place. We have a paradox at hand: the lifecycle process is one that resists change in an environment where change is an almost daily occurrence. There can be considerable disruption when products have to be produced and marketed in a short time. Rapid changes in the design, the user interface, the documentation, and marketing can be overwhelming. Why use models that are hostile to accommodating change?

Prototypes

Prototypes have emerged as a key element in software development. This gives rise to the question: *Is a prototype an alternative to the software lifecycle?* Implicit in this question are others. When is the appropriate time for a prototype? Can one prevent the prototype from becoming the actual system? Will it undermine the project in general?

A prototype, as generally conceived, is a mockup implementation of a planned system. Often limited, it may be slow to execute, have limited resources, and minimal functionality.

A related technique is what might be called a *facade implementation.* This is not a rough implementation of a system, but rather it creates the illusion of being one. For example, in a project to implement some kind of filing system on secondary storage, a facade might act as if secondary storage is used, but in all actuality implement the files in primary storage. A facade simulating a database might have some small version of the database at hand and act as if it had a complete database behind it. Similarly, a communications system might act as if messages are sent across communication lines while, in fact, it simply handles all communications internally. Both facades and prototypes have a common characteristic: they simulate a proposed system.

A prototype generally has several, but not necessarily all, of the following characteristics:

- It is a live implementation of a design.
- It can be readily modified to explore different behaviors.
- It serves as a blueprint for final production.
- It can grow in functionality to accommodate new demands.
- Speed need not be a major issue.
- It may be partially a facade (by not actually carrying out all of its apparent behavior).
- Storage requirements may be relaxed.
- It need not be fully tested.
- It may contain anomalies.

The most obvious role of a prototype is that of feasibility, especially when hardware and software are both involved. This is more or less the traditional role for prototypes.

There are other important uses as well. One of these is user testing, in which typical users (or designers) can be shown a mockup system. By observing where users have trouble, which options are little used, which keys may not be obvious to the user, the designers can modify the system accordingly.

Prototypes can be expensive to build and consume considerable resources in both personnel and equipment. On the other hand, one can be quite tolerant about its behavior. Its goal is to do something reasonable, to show feasibility, and to provide a platform for criticism and feedback. A new idea can be embodied into the prototype and tested; if its behavior is erratic on some fronts, it is not a primary concern.

One of the appeals of prototypes is that human factor issues are easily brought out into the open. Human factor specialists have long been arguing for prototypes as a means for exposing user interface deficiencies. They argue that if people have difficulties using the prototype it is an omen of what the future holds. If the perceived functionality doesn't match user needs, excessive features can be readily argued away.

Leon Levy [see Levy, 1984 and 1985] makes the point that once a prototype is completed, there can be room for a technique that he calls *tool-building*. The prototype is likely to expose areas where the direct implementation of code is not necessarily optimal. Special tools, code generators, table-driven subsystems, and the like may be built so as to accommodate further changes and speed the entire software coding process. Levy refers to this idea as *meta-programming*. At first the idea of writing software to ease the production of other software may seem counterproductive for a single software project, but this need not be the case. Software that reaches a customer base can ultimately have an extraordinarily long lifetime. These tools can make subsequent changes in the behavior of the system easier to effect and make the system considerably more reliable. Derivative products then become especially easy.

Note: A good exposition of prototypes within the software lifecycle is given in Richard Fairley's book, *Software Engineering Concepts*, 1985

What Can Go Wrong

The prototype idea is not without its own risks. A prototype can develop a life of its own. The prototype may appear on day three and cease to exist when the product is shipped. So much attention can be given to the prototype that the quality of what is underneath is overlooked. Too often the underlying quality of the final software is sacrificed by the attention given to the prototype.

When prototypes become too dominant, there is a risk that the prototype will turn out to be the product itself. This happens. The customer who thought that the prototype was only a prototype may have a surprise, because few of the criteria for reliability normally applied to a final product were applied to the prototype. Thus there is hardly any guarantee that the prototype will satisfy the standards of professional software. Yet, when the demand is urgent, when the deadline has already been passed, the prototype reluctantly finds its way to the customer. Revisions of such a product will be more likely and the lifetime of the product will suffer.

Even if a prototype does not become the product, another pitfall that could await the prototype developer is: an apology for poor programming practices. Because quality-related issues are not critical to a prototype developer, it is easy to proceed with the prototype even when it means sacrificing the best in programming practices. Oddly enough, it is this very environment that creates a tolerance for poor practices which, in turn, becomes the norm.

It is easy for the prototype to overwhelm the software lifecycle, so that phases become indistinguishable and the development process becomes more an unmarked continuum. This is surely an invitation to problems later on. There should be a serious user documentation stage, an implementation phase where the quality of the code is important, and a recognized and honest testing phase that minimizes changes.

The interest, then, lies in the prototype—not on the initial estimates, the scheduling of resources, or the building of an integrated test set. Benchmarks only get in the way. The consequence can be an unmanageable drift throughout the development cycle.

Revisiting the Software Lifecycle

Each software project has characteristics that make it unique, and one should spell out a software lifecycle to meet those special needs. If prototyping is a major part of the development cycle, it should be identified as such. It should be made visible and put into context.

Figure 3.1 is one sample lifecycle where a prototype is a major component. In particular, notice the loop within the cycle where the prototype is developed, reviewed, and revised. Revisions can occur many times and the loop may accordingly be iterated over and over again. But at some point, the prototype as a centerpiece is finished.

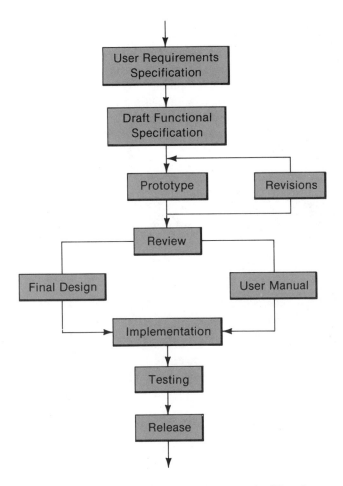

Figure 3.1 One scenario for prototyping in the lifecycle

To accommodate the software lifecycle, the initial functional specification of the system may only need to be sketched out because the prototype can ultimately serve in a specification role. The builders of the final system may have to match the prototype, not a written specification.

Whatever the values in prototypes (and there are many), they must be integrated into a software lifecycle with care and planning. That is, there still must be distinct phases with visible and testable benchmarks. These phases are completed with appropriate sign-off from management and buy-in to subsequent stages.

In conclusion,

- The software lifecyle (in whatever form is appropriate) remains the cornerstone of software development.
- The lifecycle is pre-planned with distinct stages.
- Benchmarks are clear and visible.
- Prototypes should be incorporated within (not substituted for) a software lifecycle.

Let us see how these ideas are incorporated in Sam Weber's follow-up letter, which concludes this chapter.

COMPUTER AUDITS, LTD.

Highrise Building   •   *New York, New York*   •   10023

August 4, 1986

William B. Smythe, Program Manager
DeltaSoft Products, Inc.
11 Technology Circle
Boston, MA 02114

Dear Bill:

SUBJECT: FOLLOW-UP LETTER—PROJECT SPREAD-CALC

We were gratified to receive a prompt response to our audit letter of July 14; my secretary said she bet we would hear from you within a week and she was right! It indicates, to your credit, your concern over Spread-Calc in its present status and your reluctance—however necessary you think it may eventually be—to consider organizational changes. I should like to respond to (1) your criticism of the software lifecycle and (2) your questions about prototypes.

As I wrote before, Spread-Calc, in particular, has few visible signs of the software lifecycle. Thus it may be beneficial if I make a few addenda to our cover letter of July 14th, especially now when I gather you are seriously thinking about launching Spread-Calc II.

Remember, Bill, the important element of a software lifecycle is planning. Each stage produces a certain output and prepares for the next stage. Start thinking "up-front"—i.e., up-front work is needed for several items, including:

1. the schedule
2. a functional specification
3. the documentation set
4. the commitment of resources
5. organizational strategy
6. testing methods

For example, the functional specification itself is a tough hurdle to jump. Many months may pass before a single line of code is written. The process will try your patience and the patience of your senior programmers because this kind of planning is expensive and time consuming. But in light of your current experience with Spread-Calc, you might agree that planning is what you lacked.

Page 2
August 4, 1986

Prototypes have many uses *within* the software lifecycle (note emphasis). At the early stages, they can be used to test various critical design ideas, to see how satisfactorily the system meets basic expectations. Differences of opinion can be resolved by making limited implementations of different versions. You can then test performance either with users or with a given hardware configuration. In later stages, more complete kinds of prototypes can be used to define a given design and pinpoint potential trouble spots.

Another use for prototypes is promotion. Customers can be exposed to the system before delivery and determine whether it meets their requirements. Sales departments can have a better idea of what is about to be built, and management can have a clearer idea of what the entire project is about.

So, prototypes are important. The product can be seen, even in its embryo stages. Fuzzy ideas about the design can be clarified and the more difficult problems are often exposed early. Importantly, users, developers, and critics can all interact with something that might resemble the final system.

There is no doubt that prototypes are gaining credibility in software development because they often serve as the basis around which the entire development cycle occurs. But are prototypes an alternative to the software lifecycle? Let's see.

For some, unfortunately (and this is my argument), a prototype overwhelms the software development process.

You tell me, Bill, in your letter, that you had a prototype for Spread-Calc—and indeed, you did. I regret now that I didn't aim my auditing rifle more directly at this target. Quite frankly, the problem with prototyping is that it becomes an excuse for having no software lifecycle at all. Surely, from my opening remarks, you can see that it is not a case of *alternatives,* but a case of careful and proper *inclusion* of the prototype into the software lifecycle. There is no reason why prototyping cannot be both a central *feature* of project development and still conform to an orderly *method* of software development.

If you go back and look at the prototype for Spread-Calc, Bill, I think you might agree that it was beginning to achieve a life of its own. Let me conclude in examining some of the risks of prototypes and the relationships that prototypes have to the software lifecycle.

By nature, prototypes are subject to change. This is their value. But as such, prototypes become a moving target when the requirements for the software are changing on a daily basis. This rapid change can feed itself into the development cycle, even to matters unrelated to the changing software requirements. The project itself achieves a state of instability—possibly the best diagnosis of Spread-Calc. Progress on virtually any front is limited and restricted. Not only the software, but the project itself may become a moving target. This is what you've got to be thinking about, Bill, as you consider Spread-Calc II.

Yes, there are risks as I mentioned above, whether or not a prototype is being employed. These risks are:

Page 3
August 4, 1986

1. a collapse of any software lifecycle
2. using the prototype for the final product
3. developing poor programming practices (after the fact)
4. failure to establish hard benchmarks
5. putting the project on a fast-moving treadmill

None of these need be the case.

Our experience after many audits is that prototyping is a splendid idea that is probably more underused than overused. It is not a matter of one approach or the other, it is a matter of prudent integration of one good idea (prototype) into one good method (lifecycle). Don't throw away the lifecycle approach; modify it with any new tool you discover.

Yours in better programming,

Sam Weber

Sam Weber
Chief, Audit Division

4

Programming
Teams

There are large differences in the skills and competence of professional programmers. It is not an idle observation that a small group of professionals organized together will also perform collectively to vastly different standards. This phenomenon is not peculiar to programming.

Regardless of one's private view of American military operations, there is a ready analogy to be drawn between the professional programming team and the professional aerial combat crew. The focus here is not the particular objective of either team, but how they function in pursuit of their objective.

Briefly, the six members of the crew are a pilot (the crew commander), a copilot, a radar-navigator, a navigator, an electronics warfare officer, and a gunner (not shown). The crew is organized around the pilot and the radar-navigator. The training that follows the organization of each crew is directed toward making six people of varying experience, age, and aptitude into a functioning professional unit. A given crew may include the Old Pilot who likes to recall flying airplanes when "the only thing a pilot ever worried about was catching his scarf in the rudder," along with the fresh-out-of-school navigator, who has just learned that a sextant had nothing to do with reproduction. In military jargon, such a bunch is called a "gaggle" (as in *geese*). It takes time to transform a gaggle into an "exultation" (as in *larks*).

The organization of the flight crew in simplified form is illustrated in Figure 4.1. Notice that responsibilities for tasks are clearly defined. Notice also that, while the pilot is the ultimate team authority, each member supports several critical functions; and no member, not even the pilot, is involved in every function.

Teams—A Collective Goal

Amazingly, the transition from gaggle to exultation takes place because each crew member learns and accepts that a collective goal transcends individual effort. Admittedly, the first goal may be simple survival. But the primary goal is: "Let's do what we're supposed to do and do it well." It is this goal that

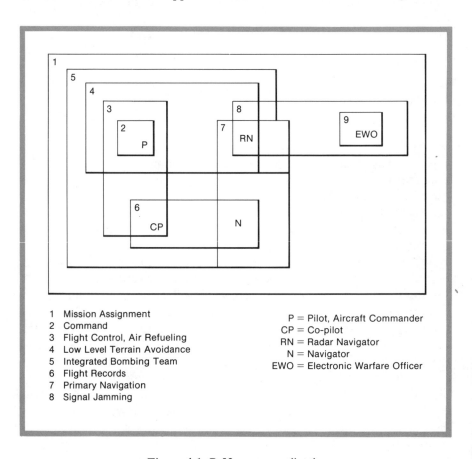

1 Mission Assignment
2 Command
3 Flight Control, Air Refueling
4 Low Level Terrain Avoidance
5 Integrated Bombing Team
6 Flight Records
7 Primary Navigation
8 Signal Jamming

P = Pilot, Aircraft Commander
CP = Co-pilot
RN = Radar Navigator
N = Navigator
EWO = Electronic Warfare Officer

Figure 4.1 B-52 crew coordination

describes the collective effort of a professional programming team. In both cases, the role of the individual member must be subservient to the larger goal of the mission or project. Each member of the crew or team must identify with the success of a collective effort.

What of programming teams? Programming, like flying, is not only a technical matter, it involves *people*. On too many programming projects, technical issues become dominant over organizational structure and working relationships.

A programming team (see Figure 4.2) is a small collection of people, usually from three to eight individuals, working on a single project. Given a choice, the smaller the team the better; if you can get by with three or four, do it. Teams are not a new or radical idea. More than a few program managers think of their programmers and support personnel as programming teams—when in fact, the project members are hardly a team but only a group. In this setting, the team concept becomes a delusion. The members fail to understand the principles of team programming and why these principles are important. Team players do what is necessary for the project to succeed, even if it does not always appear compatible with their own individual objectives. Everyone succeeds if the project succeeds.

Effective orientation towards a collective goal is a distinguishing mark of a programming team. The role of each individual member is subservient to the larger goals of the project. Each holds the success of the project as the highest benefit. The fact that one member of the team may write the documentation and another the critical algorithms is not particularly noteworthy. The noteworthy fact is that these parts of the project must integrate and drive the process as a whole. When a hardware engineer takes

Figure 4.2
Programming Groups versus Programming Teams

Marks of a group:	*Marks of a team:*
1. Individual performers	1. A collective goal
2. Responsibilities allowed to drift	2. Task-based structure
3. Organizational "meetings"	3. Frequent internal walkthroughs
4. Individual egos	4. Collective ego
5. Members have other major responsibilities	5. Major task for each member
6. Relative isolation	6. Frequent work reading

pride that his work has been completed but another's has not, when a programmer takes pride that her module works but someone else's does not—in short, when individual members thrive only on their own accomplishments—the team concept disintegrates.

Note: Much of my thinking about programming teams has been influenced by Weinberg's early book, *The Psychology of Computer Programming*. Here, in 1971, Weinberg presented an evocative view of the nature of programming. It is still effective for teaching and understanding the subtleties of team programming. A much newer work, *Becoming a Technical Leader*, [Weinberg, 1986] is a superb sequel.

Teams—An Organizational Unit

A programming team represents an exercise in handling large and often diffuse problems. This means that there must be a system for making decisions and distributing tasks. Relative individual skills are more important than any absolute criteria.

There are numerous broad organizational structures to consider, three of which are shown in Figure 4.3. Another view of the same information is shown in Figure 4.4. (In each diagram, the largest circle represents the project itself, and the smaller circles, its team members.)

The first structure in each figure is a *democratic* team. Here, decisions are made more or less on a consensus basis. There is only a minimal hierarchy of authority, although one or two members usually emerge in more leading roles. The thrust of the team, however, is toward concensus and agreement of objectives.

The democractic team tends to arise when members view themselves as more or less equal participants. Sometimes this works to the detriment of the team performance, because most software projects require a variety of different skills. For example, the best software designer may be the worst tester. The most prolific coder may be the most inept documenter. A democratic team works best when each individual has an objective view of the relative skills of all coworkers, and no task—however insignificant it seems—is viewed as beneath anyone's skills. No dignity is lost if one has to maintain the project archives. The mundane tasks have to be done and must be considered as important as the overall software design.

The second organizational structure in each figure is the *leader-based* team. Here, the team acknowledges that one member possesses substantially greater skills than any other member of the team. This member is sometimes thought of as the chief programmer.

As is so easy with any terminology, the term "chief programmer" may suggest different connotations to different people. On programming teams,

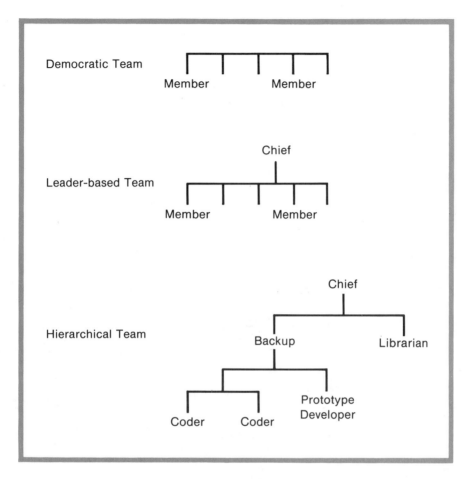

Figure 4.3 Three programming team prganizations

however, the term may not be an apt description. Chief programmers are chosen because of their ability to motivate people or because of their superior insights into the methods of software development. They may not be as skilled at every aspects of software. More often than not, they have several shortcomings; the chief programmer may not even be the best coder. But because they understand quality work, regardless of how well they themselves can perform it, chief programmers gain the respect of others. They can make sound decisions and organize people effectively.

Accordingly, the other members of the team work on the whole to support the chief. This does not mean that the other members are

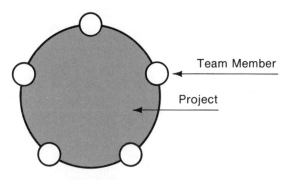

(a)   Democratic team

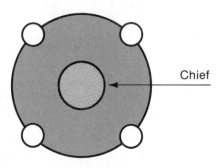

(b)   Leader-based team

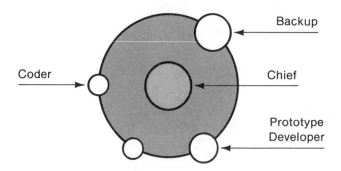

(c)   Hierarchical team

Figure 4.4 Team organization

secondary—this is a short-sighted attitude. Any aspect of software development can become the crucial aspect at the critical time. Documentation may turn out to be the key to project success or failure. There are times during development when appropriate testing and test sets will determine if the time schedule is met. The leader-based team falls apart when the leader ends up taking on almost every task and patching up the work of other members. It works best when all members respect the leader, yet still view themselves as critical partners, and are treated as such.

The third structure is a variant on the second—the *hierarchical* team. In this organization, there is a chief programmer (much as in the leader-based team), one or two subordinates, and one or more members at a lower level in the hierarchy. This is typical of the ladder or branching-tree organization in most corporations, although the designations here are chief programmer, a backup or deputy programmer, support programmer, and other members such as librarians, archivists, testers, and documenters.

The danger of this kind of team is that there is a tendency to compartmentalize every task and then, perhaps, subordinate it to a level where it is not considered to be critical. Some members may view their roles as peripheral. As the management of this team is more diffuse, communication problems among members can arise. Nevertheless, this organization can be dramatically effective, especially when the expertise of the team members varies considerably.

The so-called *surgical* or *chief programmer* team, proposed by Harlan Mills many years ago [see Brooks, 1975], has elements of both the leader-based team and the hierarchical team. For small projects, the two-level model of the leader-based team is more likely to be appropriate; each member may have a more or less fixed role; but the chain of command is directly to the chief. For large projects, a more hierarchical situation may be needed.

Teams—Specific Tasks

Not everyone on the crew can land the airplane. There are analogous issues in programming projects. Delegation of tasks is critical in any software project. But hand-in-hand with delegation must go the responsibility to see that the job is done well. In a programming team, this responsibility ultimately rests with the person who carries out the task.

It is the task, not effort, that is delegated. It may not be good to hear that "Sam and Janice are doing the I/O routines" or "All three of us are doing the design." Why? Because someone has to do the actual work and someone has to take ultimate responsibility. If Sam and Janice have a specification to work from and have jointly set a date to deliver the routines, that's fine. But if Sam and Janice each think it is really the other person's task or if no one really knows what I/O routines are actually needed, we may be creating a delusion.

It happens too often that one or two members of a programming project tend to take on more responsibility to see that the project proceeds. In itself, this would appear to be beneficial but, in so doing, the one or two team members begin to think of their responsibility as authority. This is the beginning of team fragmentation.

The team is not served if a task is done in a kind of isolation, with the results reported only at the end. The obverse of this coin, however, is that the team leader (who has the authority for the project) must recognize this kind of weakness. Consider the person delegated to documentation. It is not enough to fulfill one's own responsibility—in this case, documentation. It must be understood that the responsibility is to the team as well as to the management. Every individual on the team should be able to consider (without necessarily giving in to) the criticisms and suggestions of other team members, including the leader.

The individual doing the documentation should periodically release the documentation to other members of the programming team. They can suggest changes while the documentation is still under development. The team member should welcome this other input. There will be slips, omissions, and unfinished aspects, and some individual tasks will languish for a while. But the process is important. Counting on some final great burst of energy to complete a task because of individual pride can cause the project as a whole to suffer.

In short, on a programming team, specific tasks should be spelled out carefully and delegated to individuals. The delegation carries with it a responsibility to see that the task is done well and (hopefully) completed on time.

The Team as One's Major Activity

Software engineer Tom Smith is 40% on this project, 30% on that project, and 20% on some other task. This may be an indication that none of the three activities is organized on a team basis. Membership on a team usually requires that the project become the dominant activity for most of the individuals involved (see Figure 4.5). During the initial startup, or as the

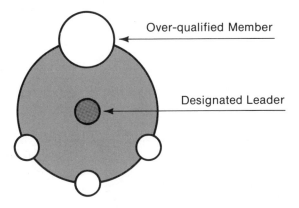

(a) Choice of inappropriate leader

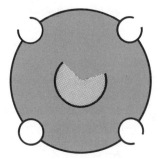

(b) Members on other projects

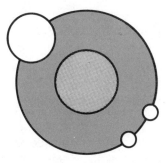

(c) Weak members

Figure 4.5 Some organizational problems on a team

project is winding down, full team participation may not be necessary. But while the bulk of the project is carried out, a more or less full-time participation is virtually mandatory.

Good programmers will usually be involved in outside efforts, for example, conferences, papers in progress, and teaching or class commitments, if only to keep abreast of the field. But there must be an authoritative definition of the composition of the team that includes a projection of time allocations for all members. It may be quite proper for Tom Smith to note a 40/30/20 distribution of his energies as previously cited, but when the project is in full swing something on the order of 75-100% of his efforts will probably be required for a specified period of time.

This problem is not difficult to overcome because it can be managed by proper planning—that is, during the organizational process. As the necessary team structure is defined, responsibilities will be delegated, and this entails considering how individual efforts are to be allocated in order to complete the project.

Choosing a Team

The choice of an appropriate organizational structure for a programming team depends on the individuals, their strengths, and their weaknesses (see Figure 4.5). Once the organizational issues are resolved, then the characteristics that affect individuals on the team can be the focus for project completion.

When the team concept in project planning is not a consideration at the onset of a software engineering endeavor, results are unpredictable. For example,

- Project managers may intrude into every phase of the project, helping little by doing so;
- Team leaders may lack the necessary personal skills;
- Team members may all seem to be doing every task;
- Program testers may find themselves motionless before a terminal for hours on end.

Such situations may not at all mean that the people are truly incompetent. Everyone possesses certain relative skills. Some are skilled programmers who are not challenged when their duties include such tasks as writing memos; others delight in simple organization and maintain superb project archives. Some are potent critics; others need guidance and are willing to accept criticism.

The challenge is to find the right role at the right time. Ideally, the general team makeup should be chosen before the first line of code is written or, even better, before the outline of the project is settled. At first, there is nothing but perceptions. As the project proceeds, these perceptions are translated into reality. There will be programmers who are considered by their peers as incompetent programmers but who, when assigned as testers, succeed where others fail. Apprentice programmers may perfer to be code readers rather than sit on the sidelines of the project—they want to be involved no matter how oblique their task may be. Others may be so well-organized at a terminal that they are perfect librarians.

Consider the following scenario:

> Frank C. is the manager of a small software project. Frank is a knowledgeable hardware engineer, but his knowledge of professional software engineering techniques is marginal. His belief is that programmers do best when left alone.
>
> Jim, the designated leader, is an articulate person, speaks well at meetings, and is a good critic of other people's work. His shortcoming is his own work, mainly one of discipline and follow-through.
>
> Brenda G. is second-in-command. Brenda is a person of quiet ways, but her work is excellent.
>
> Brian M. is assigned to write most of the code. He is a meticulous organizer of information but not very comfortable generating module after module for other people's scrutiny.
>
> Mike B. is the low man on the totem pole and is basically assigned to documentation. Mike has not had much experience writing code and is kept out of this matter.

We see in this little scenario the following general structure:

Manager (Frank C.) →
    Lead Programmer: Jim
    Backup Programmer: Brenda G.
    Coder: Brian M.
    Documentation: Mike B.

This is a scenario that will probably not work well. People have roles based on assumptions that do not match their personalities, needs for growth, and individual skills. Another organization might be as follows:

Manager (Frank C.) →
    Lead Programmer: Brenda G.
    Assistant Programmer: Mike B.
    Documentation: Jim
    Librarian: Brian M.

In this scenario, the other three basically provide extensive support roles for Brenda G. Even this team structure may not work. In fragile cases like this, the manager should take steps to review the situation periodically.

Matching the variety of human skills to those needed for effective software development is in itself a talent. That talent is best exercised in planning, but often must await the initial phase of operation to be refined and settled well.

Why Teams?

Each of the above criteria—a single goal, team structure, specific tasks, work reading and walkthroughs (discussed in a separate chapter), and the understanding of individual roles—are kinds of litmus tests to determine if a project is being developed by a gaggle of programmers or a real team of professionals (an exultation). We now turn to an underlying question: why teams?

A combat crew is purposely structured as it is because its task is specific and the training to accomplish that task is repetitive in nature. But not all flying crews are combat crews. The commercial airlines are an example where every qualified member can fly with any other individual and nothing is lost in getting the job done. So why should we have teams in programming?

On the debit side, teams may appear to be inefficient. Managers may sense a loss of control in preventing teams from squandering their time or from bickering among themselves. Moreover, when programmers and programmer-support people organize as a team, they may (and often should) demand resources that might not otherwise be given to the project.

The argument *for* teams is, first of all, an argument against drift. Responsibility can be spread across so many people that it is hard to know who is in control. Tendencies to fragment the responsibilities of a professional, shortage of key resources, and widely spread development efforts are the norm and not the exception. What the team offers is a focus for work. It centers the control of a software project in the hands of a few people. These few practitioners have responsibility for seeing that things are done. It is said that software efforts are better when conceived by a few people. That litany has been repeated in the literature, in comments from users, and in pronouncements by project management.

The team controls all technical aspects of software development, from writing the initial functional specification to the testing and delivery of the final code. To achieve integrity in this process, a few people are involved from the beginning to the end and are supported with good resources. This ensures a simplicity in the software lifecycle. It also fosters a superb training ground for learning about the entire software development process. When the development effort is fragmented, as it so commonly is, learning about the nature of software and how to produce it well becomes a lost art.

But above these reasons, I believe there are two that dominate the rest. These are *efficiency* and *quality*. The focus of a few minds, the frequent team walkthroughs, the major commitment of each individual's time, and the common goal shared by team members—these factors converge. They head in the direction of a streamlined process and a product of much higher quality than is likely to be produced by other means. In short, small programming teams are a cornerstone of software excellence.

5

The Personality Thicket

There are three small p's of professional programming: procedure, process, and personality. Each relates to on-going activities of a programming team. Although the boundaries among them are often blurred, understanding their relationships is vital for the fourth p—the project.

My experience with some software projects is that these entities are related in this manner:

$$\frac{\text{(Procedure and Process)}}{\text{Personality}} = \text{Project}$$

where, in fact, successful software is the product of this formula:

$$\text{(Procedure and Process)} \times \text{Personality} = \text{Project}$$

When personalities intrude on procedures and processes, the result is divisive and the project itself suffers by some diminishing factor. But when all three are properly oriented during software development, the result is a multiplication of individual talents.

It must be human nature to assume that things will go well. Yet, when a project suffers in midstream or someone quits or the schedule is extraordinarily late, we wonder, "What happened?" It is too quick to dismiss the matter as unavoidable. These issues are not as uncontrollable as they appear. They are partly a matter of awareness, partly managerial, and partly a matter of inspiration. Simply put, somewhere, someone may not have understood the human "factors of life."

What is the principle human issue of programming life? Change. This means not only technical change or managerial change. Change will occur as personalities collide or in the ways that one person works with another. Change will occur as the ego grows or, better, accepts the project goal. Change will occur as individuals find their place on a team. Software development demands that these behavioral (i.e., human) issues be a primary consideration, if only because they appear so often in the course of a project.

Human problems are best handled through thought awareness and prudent planning; so that as they arise, as they surely will, there are no surprises. Thinking about human issues is one method of ensuring that these kinds of individual practices will not undermine the success of the collective effort.

Note: This chapter and the previous one may be viewed as a pair, much like the twin concepts, macro-economics and micro-economics. The previous chapter discussed the macro-situation, a look at the overall issues of programming teams. This chapter treats the micro-situation, a look at the individual.

The topic of this chapter relates to Weinberg's two books mentioned earlier, *The Psychology of Computer Programming* [Weinberg, 1971] and *Becoming a Technical Leader* [Weinberg, 1986]. Weinberg's approach was a signal that we must address the human issues in software engineering as well as the data structures and algorithms.

Some Problems

In government, one way to solve a problem is to throw money at it. In programming projects, we often try to solve a problem by throwing talent at it—bringing in different people at different times, playing a kind of musical chairs by role swapping in the middle of the project. Money can help, especially if spent on support or salaries. But human problems are a separate matter. They often don't just "go away."

What are some of the problems that can arise?

Talent Overload. It is not always true that a project should be staffed with several star performers. Two pilots, regardless of their talent and experience, cannot land an airplane at the same time. Neither can success occur when two good intellects are in constant tension.

Negativism. This is an individual who, consciously or unconsciously, becomes hypercritical, finding defects with the project or the accomplishments of others. This is the "sniper" problem.

Superiority. This is the prima donna who thinks that he or she is above the established hierarchy. This attitude can disrupt any project.

Bickering. The bickering may be about a choice of fonts for a manual or about a wrong decision and who made it. This may be nothing more than a source of distraction, or a symptom of an imminent project collapse.

Singling out. This is usually a readiness to attack a particular person's work. The work may not be the best at the moment, but it won't improve with unconstructive criticism.

Complaining. We can complain about the less than optimal working conditions, but accentuating the negative will not ameliorate the situation. Complaints will ensure that Murphy's Law prevails—if anything can go wrong, it will.

Boasting. This is the programmer who spends as much time advertising his worth as he devotes to his duties. Flaunting one's talent is never helpful.

Domination. Here we have intimidation of one or two individuals whose competence never reveals itself.

Such problems are not unique to the team organization itself. They occur whenever people must work together, no matter what the organization.

Solving human problems on a project is seldom easy. The first problem is awareness itself. It may take months to see that something identifiable is clearly wrong. I may not be aware that Fred's personality is a problem for the team, or that Betty's political views are coloring her working attitude towards Mike. Even still, the issues are difficult. The specifics are more difficult. Let us look at a few possibilities.

Talent Overload. Here we have two strong egos colliding. Each is a threat to the other. What to do? First, open discussion between the two. There may be huge tacit misunderstandings. When faced, the light may come. Second, create a distance between their roles. One can work on the user interface, the other on data management. Distance will reduce collision and give time for respect to develop.

Superiority. One can let the matter go, hoping it will work out; but working in conflict with the team must be stopped. This may require a dressing down from management. It may even require removing the individual from the team, so that a completely new programming environment can be established, letting the project proceed to completion without undue difficulties.

Bickering. Let it go? Possibly, but not for too long. The project manager can take the two aside and force them to get together to discuss their differences. Amazingly, forcing the issue to the open can give mutual understanding; some adjustment can be made; and the project can often finish with no further intrusion.

Singling out. The likelihood here is that the person's work is indeed weak. It may be unwise to continue the present assignment of tasks. It is better to find a task the person *can* handle. It may have to be something like improving work conditions or running experiments, but somewhere there usually is a solution.

Domination. This situation is well worth the effort to solve. The key may be the isolation of a task that really stands on its own. If good work results, the others may see it and stop dominating.

There are many such problems (see Figures 5.1 and 5.2) and many potential solutions (see Figure 5.2). Probably as much as any aspect of software, this area requires patience and imagination.

One general point should be kept in mind whenever problems arise. If the broad objectives of a programming team are understood, the team can work toward a common goal. The ultimate rewards will rebound not only to the team for the successful completion of the project, but also to each individual on the team. Success is contagious among all who are party to it.

Personality

Quality work requires thoughtful concentration. Some of the best professional programmers are reflective, quiet—perhaps introspective in nature. They may have an effortless manner of being punctual and tidy. There is a kind of poet's soul in a programmer that seeks clarity in code as a poet seeks simplicity of line. They have the ability to submit to an inner humility when starting over is the best thing one can do.

Consider the following scenario:

Richard A. is a member of a class studying modern concepts in programming. Richard doesn't always come to class but when he does come, he is always on time. He almost never volunteers to answer a question. He becomes invisible, dwarfed by the others. A preliminary assignment is given, and

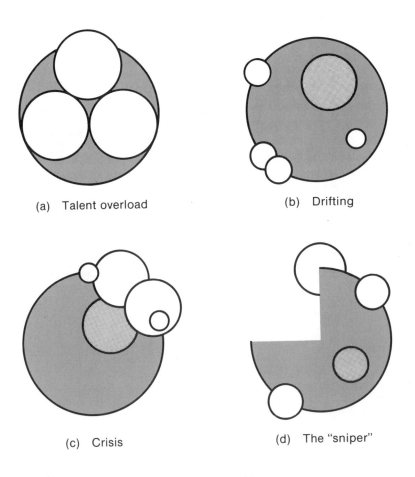

(a) Talent overload

(b) Drifting

(c) Crisis

(d) The "sniper"

Figure 5.1 Some team problems

Richard's work goes unnoticed simply because it appears on time and is of acceptable value.

A few weeks later a more challenging task is given. There is much fanfare as the work progresses. Richard again is unnoticed. Finally, the due date arrives and the pieces of work are submitted for review. In going over the work, one or two pieces stand-out. Richard's name is on one of them. I now try to recall who he is. I have been bitten by the quality of his work.

If all programmers were to fit this description, planning would be nothing more than scheduling. Quiet, hard-working talent always has a place on the team.

Figure 5.2
Some Solutions?

Problem	Possible Team Solution?	Possible Management Solution?
Weak team	Development of strict procedures	Enforcement of strict procedures
Competent but negative leader	Raise issue at an open meeting	Discussion with leader
Moderate but negative leader	Talk to management	Put in support role in next project
Weak but well-respected leader	Carry on	Put in support role in next project
Disruptive member	Quiet airing of problem	Direct confrontation or assignment to another project
Two quarreling team members	Help the team members to confront the matter	Bring issue to the open
Weak member	Try to give member well-defined tasks	Use in support roles
Very weak member	Talk to management	Remove member

If the truth be known, talent is often associated with a bright star, one who is (a bit too) radiant in speech and manner. The bright star can appear to do wonders, especially when matters are difficult. But we must be careful not to confuse the bright star with a quasar. The real bright star means talent, the quasar is unknown. The quasar may turn out to be an extrovert who talks only to cover a limited expertise.

Consider this scenario:

> The course begins and I am immediately struck by John R.'s remarks. He has already begun to question the deeper issues in programming. By the third week, there is no question that he is a thinker. He takes the lead in challenging the ideas that deserve challenging. The first small assignment comes. John R. produces it in easy fashion. The write-up supporting the assignment is long and penetrating. I begin to suspect that it may also be a bit boring, but never mind.
>
> Now comes the larger assignment. As the class proceeds and the difficult issues are exposed, John R. is always there questioning the generality of solutions and reaching for the prize.

The due date arrives. John R. produces no solution. He is working on a "more general" solution. I am happy to wait. Weeks later no solution has yet emerged. I ask to see the preliminary work. It is a mess.

These are two scenarios. There is good news and there is bad news. The good news is that the bright star may dim. In the process of association, an osmosis can take place where humility replaces arrogance. The best bright star develops the sense and tact to work easily with others. The bad news is that the naturally capable introvert can be overwhelmed and become discouraged by bright lights.

Programming groups have their share of stress, especially when the schedule is tight or approaching the absurd. My favorite kind of programming group has at least one person who is just plain fun to work with. Programming itself is a serious business, but the mental load can be lightened considerably with some good laughs. To be able to have a laugh at one's work, the machine, one's peer group, or the ridiculous constraints under which programmers sometimes work is worth much. Even a diminished bright star can make us laugh at ourselves when all around are crying. Sometimes, this may be the key to success—stop, laugh, and get cracking again.

Egoless Programming

Weinberg uses the term *egoless programming* to describe one of the most difficult attitudes to establish in a working programming environment. Egoless programming is an attitude that welcomes open comment. If the idea is perceived as an intrusion on personal egos, matters will not be resolved and the project will constantly suffer. But if the idea is considered as a procedure to overcome problems, it will ultimately lead to a straight focus on the work to be done and an eventual economy of time.

The term "egoless programming" itself is a dichotomy. On the one hand, it means being able to submit one's work to others, to listen to comments (both bad and good), and to have the enthusiasm to rework an item into which a great deal of energy may have already been expended. This extra effort means forgetting the ego contained in the original version.

On the other hand, no programming project, like any social setting, can really be egoless. A project is not a faceless Orwellian scenario. The key is that the personal ego has to identify with the collective ego. The collective ego is vital to the success of the project. If the project does succeed, the personal egos, in turn, will be the great beneficiaries.

Egoless programming is a difficult attitude for some to adopt. The idea of exposing one's work to one's peers and actually inviting their free comments can become an emotional issue. The best professional programmers, on the other hand, welcome the chance to have feedback on their work, realizing that it is *they* who gain.

Whether it is fear of repercussion or the simple assumption that programming is a private activity, open discussion of individual work is a major hurdle in implementing an egoless programming environment. If it is apparent that personal conflicts are the result of conflicting egos, something has to be done. Management may have to step in.

A misconception about egoless programming is that it concerns only procedural problems such as debating which identifiers will be used in a program or where to put comments. The goal of an egoless environment is to exchange substantive ideas. The ideas might relate to the schedule, data structures, or the programming conventions that pervade the entire project. The sooner this kind of interchange takes place, even when the project is in its scruffiest stage, the more likely it is that problems can be solved.

Gathering a team of diverse personnel together is no easy task. But before putting a pen to paper or finger to keyboard, it is wise to establish an attitude toward egoless programming. Once everyone understands that they need not fear criticism or be reluctant to give it, a feeling of trust will be established. The conflicts that occur, as they certainly will, are more likely to be resolved to everyone's satisfaction. Planning an egoless programming environment can make a difference. Weinberg's idea is still vital today.

Can Programmers Get Better?

We have thus far treated programmers as though the situation were static.

Some support the view that "It's the people that count" or, put another way, "Just give me good people, that's all that really counts." The implication here is that the key to successful software is choosing the right people, i.e., good software engineers. Good things happen for good people, things go wrong without them.

In opposition we have a "management view." Its corresponding cliches go like this: "It's good management that counts. Successful software is well-managed software." The implication here is that by instituting the right procedures through strong management, all will be well. The choice of people is subservient to the way a project is organized.

It is not a question of choosing between these two apparently conflicting views—it is a matter of understanding that there are important values in both. The strength of the management approach is that planning will be uppermost. On the other hand, it is unlikely that the very best of people will succeed with poor management

This does not address our question, however. Can programmers get better? Is there a dynamic involved in the total programming project that suggests individual improvement? Can an amateur programmer become a professional programmer? Can programmers adapt to the discipline of a good software lifecycle? Can management techniques channel the energies of programmers in the proper direction?

The answer to these questions is an unqualified "yes." Why? Because the sum of individual abilities is not as great as the talent of a collective unit. Individuals can write code, design proposals, and estimate resource requirements. But what can happen once immersed into a project with realistic dates and well-identified, measurable benchmarks? What happens when one has to write a complete user manual before coding or prepare an airtight functional specification? What happens? The amateur approaches the professional and a few professionals approach the master.

Improving performance is not only a matter of management. One must be exposed to good ideas. Training is essential. This can mean time and expense. One needs to take time to study issues and understand new tools. This also means bringing in people of excellence to set the record straight and getting teachers whose knowledge of software is both subtle and substantive.

6

Work Reading
and
Walkthroughs

The description of a programming team in a previous chapter describes a coordinated team of professionals whose success demands that each individual effort is known and understood by all other members of the team. From initial specification to final release, success depends upon each member contributing what he or she can, even in areas where one's expertise is limited.

Note: I have seen the word "walkthrough" used in various ways. Like the phrase "structured programming," it means different things to different people. Some sources use the word in the context of external reviews. In the discussion to follow, it is used for an internal process and the word "walkthrough" does seem just right. For some clarification, I will use the term "team walkthrough."

Work Reading

Too frequently, those who are working on one particular task tend to become protective. Their work becomes unassailable in terms of technique or expression. It becomes unthinkable that another team member (especially one working on documentation or the archives) can offer ideas to modify or improve the work. Suddenly, we find a member of the programming team on an ego trip. The admixture of a personal ego into an egoless operation will produce some drama, probably trauma.

Open discussion is alien to many. The first reaction is likely to be defensive. Individual egos must be balanced with something higher: a *collective* ego. The first is normal human nature; the second is necessary for the project. As one realizes that one's own special talent may not be enough for the project at hand to succeed, the gut response will not be that "*I* can do it" but "*We* can do it." Precocious programmers have to adopt what appears to be an unnatural stance—trading the personal for the collective ego. But once the stance is adopted, success is imminent.

A key to this situation—and it should not be a procedural placebo given lip service at the beginning of a project and ignored throughout it—is *work reading*. Work reading is an informal review of another's work. Work reading is a procedure that should be understood as a frequent and timely function in software development. Normally, work readings occur at least once or twice a day, maybe more, and often at afternoon coffee breaks:

"What you think of this?"
"Better than before, but why don't you...?"
"O.K. And how are you getting on with...?"
"Good. Check with you later?..."

And so forth. Nobody's individual ego is sacrificed, but the collective ego will be doubled if not squared. Work readings are not counter to human behavior, but a desirable extension of it. If four eyes are better than two, than why not six if necessary?

Work reading goes like this.

1. *A piece of work is prepared.* The work can be an outline of a document, a plan for new office space, the draft of a screen layout, or a list of prompting messages. It can be just a tentative sketch or in next-to-final form.
2. *The work is given to a colleague.* Usually the colleague will be someone who works on the same project, but this is not necessary. It can be anyone who might have something useful to report: a customer, a marketing person, a secretary, or an expert.
3. *The work is reviewed.* It is best when the work is reviewed as a conscious task, but a focused coffee break is fine. It is also best if written notes and comments are given so the author of the work will have a reminder. Comments of any and all variety should be made. These can range from: "The format is quite cluttered" to "I don't believe it will work."

4. *The review is given to the author.* It is vital that the author listen to all remarks. A remark like "the format is quite muddled" may give the author a new enthusiasm towards a splendid layout. A remark like "the organization is muddled," may, days later, spur an entirely new approach. One like "I don't believe it will work" may be ignored, or, weeks later, cause a faulty effort to be abandoned, with great benefit to all.

There will be times when work reading need not be frequent, and other times when it will be needed often. The point is: if it is understood at the outset that work readings are a part of software development, no one need be concerned about their role as individuals nor have any compunction about having their egos assaulted from within. The goal is to protect the integrity of the project from the slings and arrows from without.

Team Walkthroughs

Not in opposition to, but complementing work reading, is the process of team walkthroughs (see Figure 6.1). The team walkthrough is a scheduled event, a part of the process of developing software. It is surely not as frequent as a work reading, but it involves the programming team, sometimes in parts, sometimes all together. As a scheduled event—maybe every day—it requires some preparation. Indeed, the result is often the same as a work reading—in the end, useful modifications and improvements are ready to be made.

A team walkthrough is a brief gathering of two or more team members to review a piece of work for which someone has responsibility. The object of the team walkthrough is to discover procedural flaws, inconsistencies, or missing elements. It is not a review of the people, it is a review of the work.

Figure 6.1
Work Reading versus Team Walkthroughs

Work Reading	*Team Walkthroughs*
1. Unscheduled	1. Scheduled
2. Work based	2. Work based
3. Variable length	3. 5-10 minutes per item
4. Frequent	4. About once a day
5. Individually oriented	5. Team Oriented

The team walkthrough is prearranged and brief. Ten minutes per item is excellent. A walkthrough should seldom last more than half an hour per item. Scheduling a walkthrough in advance (even on a few hours' notice) gives the members of the programming team time to review their own progress and ascertain the progress of others. One is able to determine the status of the project without having "another long meeting," the bane of organizational progress.

The Air Force equivalent of a team walkthrough is the daily "stand-up" meeting. The implication is clear. People rarely talk too long when they are standing. The meeting is part of the routine schedule and lasts only long enough for everyone attending to know what is happening. After the session, walkthrough or stand-up, those in attendance return to business apprised of what has happened and what has to be done. The status of the project may change so quickly that the next walkthrough will be just as important for team vitality as the last. And so it proceeds until the software is developed— or so it should.

A team walkthrough could go like this:

A team member offers on item for review. The item is normally a piece of work in progress. It may be a hand-sketched draft of the schedule, a preliminary design, an outline of a data structure, or a piece of code. Usually there will be handouts.

The team member makes a few remarks. These can be a quick summary or a status report, but brevity (two minutes) is vital.

The floor is opened for discussion and comment. Criticism, ideas, and suggestions are taken collectively. The purpose is to listen, to learn— then on to the next item.

The purpose of the team walkthroughs is not to solve problems but to identify them. Sometimes the meeting ends with the brief benediction, "We're right on target...see you next time." Happiness. But more often than not, necessary follow-ups are proposed for the next walkthrough. This is a healthy scenario.

My experience with various projects, however, suggests that team walkthroughs are generally unsuccessful. As a project heats up and a deadline approaches, walkthroughs are not routinely scheduled and, ultimately, they are abandoned.

Too often, there is confusion about the difference between a walkthrough and a general meeting. The former is a work briefing; the latter is a forum, where aspects of the project can be discussed at length. Too often the team walkthrough is chosen as an opportunity to focus on the inconsequential or the tangential. Time is squandered, the walkthrough becomes a meeting, and the whole idea of brevity as a means for simple information exchange loses its appeal.

Neither is the team walkthrough a "review," where a piece of work is subjected to managerial comment. A review tends toward elaboration and prognosis for the benefit of management. The team walkthrough is just the opposite. It is an *internal* mechanism by which the programming team considers the progress of the project in a free spirit of cooperation. Management need not—indeed, must not—be present.

Team walkthroughs require discipline. The best way to approach discipline is to begin the team walkthrough process at the early stages of development. The first team walkthroughs may be only a matter of discussing a rough sketch of a project's schedule or presenting some scruffy pages outlining the overall function of the system. In midstream, the team walkthrough may be used to discuss one- or two-sentence outlines clarifying the role of each member of the team. At the end of the project, team walkthroughs may be used to review a few pages of code or a final test result.

The failure of team walkthroughs seems to reflect a failure to develop efficient work habits more than anything else—that is, it represents a failure of internal discipline. More often than not, discipline fails when the pressure is on, as the deadline approaches. But herein lies the value of the team walkthrough. Its major purpose is to detect errors *before* they arise. As the team walkthrough is adopted as a formal procedure and work reading as an informal procedure—I believe that both are under-recognized team programming principles—the result can only be a more professional product.

Work reading and team walkthroughs are two procedures that knit the fabric of a team together. It may very well be that only the pilot lands an aircraft, but it takes the entire crew to find the runway.

"LA VOILÀ . . . MA MAISON DE CAMPAGNE."

7

Misconceptions
in
Human Factors

This is a true story (edited for a general audience):

> My friend, Charlie, is a free-lance writer. Several years ago, he gave in to all the editorial reports and, on the recommendation of a colleague, bought a small computer and a letter-quality printer. The package included four major elements: a filer program, a "calc" spreadsheet system, a programming method (Basic, in this case), and a word-processing program—for which he was ready to sell his typewriter. On our scale of programming expertise, Charlie was an amateur and there only in the field of word processing. This is what happened.

> His was not the most popular computer, but the advice given to him was that it deserved to be recognized as a quality product that would serve him in good stead. Sent home with a battery of user manuals, he began the process of learning word processing with the computer.

> One of the user manuals was a collection of engineering documents compiled in no particular order. As one who fancies the use of language to communicate rather than impress, Charlie was unable to gather any intelligence from the manual. He came close to tears trying to interpret the last chapter, "Dynamic Debugging Tool."

> Charlie had no idea why one key was used with another to do a task. At first, Charlie needed a little guide beside him to remind him to use "Control S," "Control C," or "Escape Q" at the right time. He noticed an advertisement for a

template that fit on the keyboard, but he wanted to memorize the necessary commands so that he would not have to "think" about key combinations.

When Charlie decided to use the filer program, the keys for certain functions for filing were different from those for the same situation in the word processing program. And when he tried the "calc" program, thinking he might make sense out of a family budget with a marvelous spreadsheet, he had to employ a third set of command keys.

Using the computer for document preparation, Charlie completed a little historical research project nine months after he purchased the computer. He could confidently say that, with the aid of an independently written user manual that he bought off the shelf of a local bookstore, he was ready to give his typewriter away to his kids at college—which he did.

Two years later, a friend suggested that they collaborate on a book. The problem would be simplified if Charlie used a new word processing program with a new computer. By interfacing the two with a modem, they could exchange completed portions of the manuscripts readily.

But Charlie declined. "You must have gone bananas if you think I'm going to learn another word processing program—and I don't think you have the time or perseverance to learn mine!"

This little story is not unlike others I have heard. But what is Charlie's trying little experience all about?

It is about human factors. It is about the eyebrow-lifting phrase "user-friendly." With a few exceptions, (for instance, the simple, clean design of Macintosh Pascal), I believe that we have lost touch with the deeper human factor issues in software. Here is a brief taxonomy of human engineering problems:

- A maze of conventions
- Lack of technical elegance
- Complexity of individual keystrokes
- Menu confusion
- Second-rate documentation
- Obscure, system-based output
- Intolerance to error
- Special key syndrome
- Cluttered screens

It is appropriate to consider what "user-friendly" really means.

In the discipline of computer science, there is a distinction to make. This is between the foundational approach that is necessarily quantitative, and a qualitative aspect that shapes our work. In particular, for human factors, there are qualitative questions that have to be addressed:

What are human factors and how important are they?

Who knows what they are? Rather, who *should* know what they are? Users? Software engineers? Psychologists? Or designers?

What considerations should the programmer give to low-level interface issues (such as prompts and messages)?

This aspect of programming is also called *human engineering* or *man-machine interface.*

As a design method, human engineering adopts a set of concerns that takes into serious account the characteristics of the human user. By definition, it assumes that the human user has limitations in memory and skills. On the other hand, human engineering respects the user for having intelligence and a kind of logic that is needed to perform useful work. In sum,

Human engineering is an attitude that places the user first.

There are, I believe, some major misconceptions about human factors that pervade the field of software engineering. Some are given in Figure 7.1. They are largely unspoken, and may reflect a set of established attitudes in our profession.

Misconception 1: The Primary Goal Is to Help Novices

A novice is a user who has no particular experience with automation. When we design systems, we often ask how Charlie, the novice, would cope with it. When we document the system, try to write manuals, provide on-line help, or introduce special keys, the novice is on our minds. In short, when human

Figure 7.1
Some Tacit Misconceptions about Human Factors

1. The primary goal is to help novices.
2. Ease of learning implies ease of use.
3. Users should help design systems.
4. Menus are easier to use than commands.
5. Human engineering centers on a few key design issues.
6. Users will be comfortable with subsets.
7. Human engineering is not particularly a technical matter.
8. Human factors are chiefly a matter of taste.

factors are considered, the discussion seems to gravitate to the humble novice.

A consequence of this attitude is that, subconsciously, we think of human factors as babying the user. As an aside, notice a looming contradiction—the system evolves towards greater complexity, yet we add even more complexity (on-line help, special features) to "help" the novice. Moreover, the real workhorse systems, which are not particularly for novices, can have the worst human factors.

The marketplace is alive with computer systems: electronic mail networks, word processors, application packages, and implementations of computer languages. The people who use these systems are not primarily novices. When a new system is introduced, those who encounter it are certainly first-time users of the new system. But most of them have probably had experience with other systems and similar pieces of software. They will be transferring their skills from a previous experience to a new one; in other words, they are "transfer users" [see Good et al., 1984].

Charles the Reluctant would no doubt be able to transfer his knowledge of his own word processing system to a new one. Had he done so, Charlie's concerns as a transfer user (see Figure 7.2) would be substantially different from that of Charles the Novice. Transfer users are familiar with automation, command languages, and screen layouts. They are familiar with the small details needed in using a system—how to use special keys, invoke a command, or save work. Such users need no babied approach to the documentation or the software itself. They simply want to get on with a system that they believe will be an improvement over the old.

Even the novice may not remain novice very long. In Charlie's case, the combination of learning a command language (a fault in the design of the computer) and the need to learn a word processing program without any help

Figure 7.2
Differences between Users

The Novice	The Transfer User
Is unsure of automation	Knows what automation is
Needs encouragement	Wants to get work done
Develops skill slowly	Becomes skilled rapidly
Needs gentle documentation	Needs a good reference manual
Is hesitant with new combinations	Thrives on technical consistency

from either the dealer or the manual—all contrived to slow the learning process. But often, people are taken with the novelty and challenge. They become "experts" in a short period of time, even when complexity interferes with useful work.

The point is that spreadsheet or compiler, novice or expert, the human factors in day-to-day usage are the issues that really count.

Misconception 2: Ease of Learning Implies Ease of Use

Systems can be designed that are easy to learn or, at the very least, can incorporate additional learning features that help a user to avoid major stumbling spots. Even if the system is overly complex, it is possible to add learning aids so that the user can get started doing useful work. These examples come to mind: an extensive help facility, synonyms for command names, an assortment of tutorials, and a menu facility with considerable explanatory backup. I do not necessarily recommend these compensation practices, but we can partly make up for shortcomings with learning aids.

Nonetheless, the central and more difficult task is to design a system that from the beginning is so transparent that the uninitiated user learns effortlessly. A system is easy to *learn* if the uninitiated user can do something useful in the first hour.

Now consider the user who more or less understands overall system operation and has become reasonably proficient in dealing with it. The system is easy to *use* if the user can accomplish a task with little effort. This means no surprises, no confusion about what to do next, no frustration in retyping command lines that contain a simple error, and so forth. In short, the system helps rather than interferes with the user's work.

The question is: Does ease of *learning* imply ease of *use?* Probably not. I do not want to imply that the two goals are incompatible. But satisfying the ease-of-learning goal does not necessarily mean that ease of use has been achieved.

Attention is often focused on ease of learning. This concern is indeed a good one. But it should not disguise the fact that ease of learning is not the whole game. It is part of the problem but can readily become a misleading issue.

Misconception 3: Users Should Help Design Systems

The goal of human engineering is to support the user. The problem is how to do it. We certainly want to observe how users make use of the system—to notice their errors, observe their behavior patterns, and help them perform their tasks. The problem is that users often have no clear idea exactly what techniques, what features, and, more importantly, what larger designs actually work in practice. Because of a lack of experience, users can be their own enemy. They often call for more and more features to accommodate the application. Yet the best solution may be to out-think the problem, out-think the application, and provide a simple set of features that integrate into a simple whole.

Designing a system that meets user needs is a sophisticated and difficult task. It can only be accomplished by experts who have creative ideas, who have spent years observing users, and who understand the deeper issues in human engineering. Human engineering is a matter of skill, taste, and judgment. These skills do not come overnight. In short, the user should be the center of design, but the design should come from experienced system designers.

Misconception 4: Menus Are Easier to Use Than Commands

There is a perception that menus are easier to use than typed commands. There is a similar perception that icons (that is, visual images on the screen) and special purpose keys are also easier to learn and use. In short, command languages seem to fall in last place from an ease-of-use standpoint.

When talking about command languages, each of us has some idea of what a "command" looks like. To some, commands may suggest forms like

```
SAVE datafile := newdata      -- saving a file
REPLACE /xxx/yyy/;*           -- global replace of xxx
```

These commands have a notational style of syntax. On the other hand, one could imagine commands like

```
SAVE datafile AS newdata
CHANGE ALL "xxx" TO "yyy"
```

which have a more prose-like syntax.

In comparing various styles, one must also take into account the various ways of embodying a given style. Obviously a good menu strategy is superior to a poor command language. A set of well-orchestrated special purpose keys is superior to a poorly designed menu strategy. But let us assume the same level of excellence, obscurity, or kind of thinking in comparing a menu strategy to a command strategy.

Consider the following hypothetical menu:

```
USE DIRECTORY
FILING FUNCTIONS
PAGE CONTROL
CALCULATION
EDITING FUNCTIONS
DATA PROCESSING
MAIL
MANUAL
```

Such a menu might appear at the top level of an office automation system. Its intent is to steer the user into one of the major subsystems for further action.

There are difficult issues here (see Figure 7.3). First of all, does the list of eight menu choices completely cover the system? That is, are there other applications or subsystems available to the user? The menu implies that there are no other choices, but the fact may be otherwise.

Looking more closely at the menu, we also see a language issue. The first entry is a verb phrase, while the second entry is a noun phrase, and the fourth is a simple noun. The last entry is ambiguous. Most menu systems have these kinds of problem; it is difficult to design a consistent, clear syntax.

Wording is also difficult. Consider the phrase EDITING FUNCTIONS. The word FUNCTIONS implies a library of routines. What is probably meant here is a generalized text editor, not a set of predefined mathematical functions. The editor probably uses special purpose keys (not function calls) to enter and correct text.

The meaning of FILING FUNCTIONS and USE DIRECTORY is likewise unclear. Files might be stored in a directory. Does the directory include file names?

Figure 7.3
Some Issues with Menus

1. Covering all possibilities.
2. Consistent phrasing.
3. Choosing the right words.
4. Appropriate grouping.
5. Choosing what to include.
6. Going from one menu to another.
7. Showing how menus relate.
8. Providing needed data.

Do the filing functions allow someone to look at the directory? And if one is editing a file, does one use FILING FUNCTIONS or EDITING FUNCTIONS?

Notice the order of the items. The directory, filing, and editing choices seem to go together, but they are not listed together. The calculator, an odd item on the list, is stuck in the middle. The most frequently used function on this menu may be the mail option, and this is in seventh place. Moreover, those who are only mail users can (subconsciously) become intimidated by being constantly reminded of features they do not understand.

Now suppose we choose FILING FUNCTIONS and a second menu appears:

```
SAVE FILE
SAVE FOLDER
SAVE AS
COPY
FORMAT
NEW
RENAME
LIST OPTIONS
MANUAL
```

Here we have two verb phrases, then an incomplete phrase, then a verb, then a word that could be a noun or a verb, and an adjective all by itself.

At various times, are all these options valid? For example, if I have just entered the system, it may not make sense to save a file. If I want to look at an existing file to do further work, it is not clear whether I should select COPY or NEW. Apparently LIST OPTIONS describes further options one can choose before proceeding. But why list the options if I can get them by selecting the correct choice anyway?

There is reason to believe that there are more choices available than are listed. For instance, how do I get back to the main menu? Can I make a direct transfer? What if I choose the wrong menu option and am greeted with a question that is irrelevant to my task? This is a common circumstance in all but the simplest menu systems. In a forest of choices, am I confined to a tree-like structure or can I jump from one branch to the other? And how do I get out of the entire forest when I'm stuck?

Menus are truly a valid design choice. They are attractive in many different settings. However, they do create their own problems. For a system with only 20 or 30 possible choices in all, the menu structure is easily handled. But for more complex systems, menus are not a blank check. We should weigh their merits with command languages and any other general design strategies.

Misconception 5: Human Engineering Centers on a Few Key Design Issues

The choice of a menu strategy or a command strategy is one of the major design decisions in a system. Other major choices are the size of the screen, the method of cursor movement, whether to have on-line help, how to deal with multiple windows on a screen, and so on. These decisions are important because they are fully visible to the user who encounters the system.

The misconception is the belief that once these decisions are made the major requirements of human engineering have been met. On the contrary, the myriad of follow-on details can so overwhelm any broad design strategy that the human factors are lost.

Consider the simple use of the return key. This key is normally used to terminate a line of input text. It is also often used as a kind of "do it" key to initiate actions. It can also be used for indicating acknowledgments, terminating data entry to an application program, moving down the screen to a new line, and supplying a default response, such as "yes" for a "yes-no" question.

Such overloading of the return key can mean that users may become confused. "Do I hit the return key or not?" This issue is important because the return key is featured in every interaction with every user at every session at the keyboard. It is one of the most pervasive issues in design.

Another "detail" is the abbreviation rule used to enter command words. One common abbreviation rule states: *Any keyword can be abbreviated by one or more initial letters as long as the initial letter sequence distinguishes it from all other keywords.* For instance, if we only had the keywords,

```
REFORMAT
READ
SEND
PRINT
RUNOFF
```

then we could use these abbreviations:

```
REF
REA
S
P
RU
```

This rule requires a user to know all the keywords in the system in order to remember the shortest abbreviation. In practice, the user generally does not know all of the keywords but will eventually abstract some informal rules that tend to do the job. In the above case, the user might conclude that typing three letters for any word beginning with R is sufficient to do the job and go ahead with three letters, even for the keyword RUN. This is a situation that produces uncertainty and intimidation in the mind of the user.

There are many other such details of design—the prompting symbol or prompting message for user input, the method for selecting menu items (for example, by number, by letter, or by cursor movement), the keys for correcting small typing errors, the initial user dialogue, or the conventions for printing a file. These so-called details can have great impact on the user because their frequency of use is so high—all users face them all the time.

Look at it this way. The prompting symbol on certain popular systems is the letter naming a device drive followed by a greater-than sign, for example,

    A>

This use of the greater-than sign is an obtrusive prompt; yet, it has probably been printed more times than we can imagine. This is hardly a passing detail.

Misconception 6: Users Will Be Comfortable with Subsets

The popular wisdom is that small systems are desirable. Yet, systems have a tendency to grow anyway. How can we limit the seemingly unlimited demands of competing design forces for more features? It is nearly impossible because when a system design begins to snowball by its own momentum the subsetting idea becomes increasingly attractive. The subset idea is simple—users will pick and choose their own features, eventually establish a reasonable selection, and then will be comfortable with it. So what's wrong with large systems anyway?

There are many arguments against large scale in computer systems. Some of them have to do with cost. Others have to do with documentation and the difficulty of implementing large systems. One should question every feature in a system. Users may not need so many options if the system does the simple tasks it is designed to do, and do them well. Nevertheless, what is really wrong with the subset idea from the *user's* point of view?

Using a system well requires documentation. A system that is larger than a user needs forces the user to face a document describing many things that are irrelevant to the problem at hand. Charlie had no use for a magic "debugging tool" when he was learning his new system. Irrelevant information intimidated him. He might well have muttered: "Oh, Lord! Thy system is so big and Thy user is so small."

Moreover, the larger the system the more likely that the documentation will be inadequate. Manuals are pieced together under increasing pressure. The examples become sterile; the text uninteresting. The documentation can deteriorate into nothing more than the reports of one engineer to another. The result is a general loss of quality.

No designer can predict which part of a system a user will be using. Any system responses, help frames, or menus can only force upon the user information about unknown topics. There will also be operations, such as program configurations or file options, that some users will barely understand. The user may get lost taking an unknown option and wind up in a dead end, not knowing whether to recover or begin again. Even when the user is on the right track, the system is less likely to give the kinds of specific information that the user really needs.

Users feel most comfortable when they understand everything they see: the menus, the icons, the commands, the options, and the messages. They find themselves at ease when they believe they are in complete control. It is similar to feeling comfortable driving one's own car rather than another's. When we understand all the controls and are able to use them confidently, driving is safer, easier, and certainly less stressful. That is why Charlie eschewed templates pasted on his keyboard—he wanted his fingers to move around the keys without having to think about it.

But now for the substantive question: Why can't users simply find their own subsets and function there conveniently? In response, I ask: Whose subset? How do I get the document for the subset that I use? How can I disregard instructions on the screen that are of no relevance? What about my specific needs? Can I grow with the system or must I grope with it? Can I be sure that the subset I'm using is optimum? Am I ignorant of better ways to do what I am doing now?

The point is: If I am not comfortable with a subset, I want to learn until I am satisfied that I truly understand the system. If I cannot do this, if I finally give up exploring, I will reluctantly hold on to my subset but with a feeling of misgiving. Is this what human engineering is all about?

If this is so, the system will always seem bigger than I am and my subset is a myth.

Misconception 7: Human Engineering Is Not Particularly a Technical Matter

Few human factors specialists would agree with the above statement, but my guess is that some system developers secretly believe it. Some liken human factors to things like making system messages more pleasing for the user to read.

If human factors are important, they should be a concern from the beginning to the end of the software lifecycle. Even when the requirements for a proposed system are being sketched, human factors arise quickly. Questioning the need for features, scaling down the requirements, and looking for clean technical solutions that will meet the needs of the user— these have human factor implications.

In developing a good technical design, one must consider factors like:

- Do we need so many special purpose keys?
- How should commands or menus be organized?
- How should screen management work?
- What notations should be used?

When the design is started, there may be conflicting principles to resolve. Perhaps some experiments may need to be run to test competing ideas. Data can be gathered on an existing system to see which features are the most confusing. If an on-line help system cannot be developed in a reasonable manner, perhaps the matter should be dropped and other avenues of user training explored. Cursor movement, file management, and command language principles must be discussed and implemented as an integral part of human factors.

Let us suppose we are designing a new system for compiling, running, and testing programs. Suppose we have identified two hundred or so functions (commands, options, features, etc.). Some typical functions might be:

1. Put the compiler output in a file.
2. Recompile a single module.
3. Set a breakpoint.
4. Display the value of an expression.

Consider these questions:

- What is a good syntax model?
- Is there a consistent syntax for options?
- Which are commands versus subcommands?
- Which features can be sensibly grouped?
- Should commands be combined?
- Should all options have a default?
- Can features be grouped under a single option?

These are technical issues that directly affect the user, ease of learning, recall, and documentation.

Human engineering is not something that can be grafted on to an existing system. It is the fiber of technical development.

Misconception 8: Human Factors Are Chiefly a Matter of Taste

This argument arises in different contexts. The gist of it is that what is fine for you may not be fine for me. It all boils down to a matter of personal preference. When the pressure is on, this attitude creeps in and human factors are left behind. Or is the argument true? Let us look at some examples.

Cursor Movement—On some systems, cursor movement is irregular; that is, there are bursts of speed followed by delays or a creeping movement. Some users may be bothered by this irregularity. It is easy to overshoot when the cursor is temporarily delayed, or fall short when the cursor is temporarily fast and the button is prematurely released.

Is this a matter of taste? Certainly not. We need to work to find an appropriate and consistent speed that satisfies almost all users.

Screen Management—Imagine for the moment that you want to release storage space. You are not exactly sure which files are current, so you call for a listing of your files. There are 20 files, and the list fits comfortably on the screen. You notice two or three files that you can delete. When you go to the menu for file deletion, the list of files previously on the screen disappears. Oops! The menu has replaced the file list. You can't remember what the file names were or exactly how they were spelled.

Is this a taste issue? Again, no. It is a matter of politeness and knowing human limits.

Muscle Stress—On many systems, cursor movement and item selection are done with a mouse. When a section of text is highlighted or when windows are moved, the button must be held down until the operation is completed. Because it is easy to release the button prematurely and lose the entire operation, most users will put more pressure on the button than is otherwise needed. This is a normal human reaction. But what is the result? With repetitive use, over prolonged periods of time, one's arm and neck will be subject to undue muscle stress. This is not a taste issue.

Screen Layout—Suppose we have some latitude about where to put a particular collection of information on the screen. In a game-playing program we may want the playing board displayed in the upper left-hand corner of the screen, the center of the screen, or the bottom of the screen. Similarly, we may designate an area of the screen in which to report results or error messages. This can be across the top of the screen, in the upper right-hand corner, or down at the bottom.

Are these decisions a matter of taste? I think not. The answers are not simple, however, because they depend on other matters in system design. There will be some elements of taste but much more of logic. Most systems require a host of features that must somehow harmonize together. Whether or not we put the board in the upper left-hand corner of the screen may depend quite markedly on other factors, for instance, whether there is room for a game history. Collectively, these decisions may interact in subtle ways. One reasonable way to determine a good positioning strategy is to test the matter with potential users. There, in the context of related decisions, we can observe which general scenario seems to work best. My guess is that more often than not, one or more choices will emerge as superior.

Conclusion

When the topic "human factors" is mentioned, some mental response comes to mind. Consider this list:

1. Easy to read messages
2. Good on-line help
3. Icon and windows
4. Using a mouse
5. Simplicity

One of these items may have come to your mind.

I know people for whom item (1) is the response. Certainly, readable messges are a part of human engineering. But are they a large part? No. This is precisely what is wrong about (1) as a response. To think about human factors in this way is a misconception, and a rather deeply rooted one.

Ah, you say, do not be foolish. No one would given the definition: "Human factors is the study of writing clear messages." I agree. But the point is our misconceptions are more subtle. They affect our attitude, our work. A person who relates to item (1) is more likely to think of human factors as window dressing, an add-on to development; on the other hand, he or she will probably not articulate this view.

This is probably a consequence of being in a field that is considered "motherhood and apple pie." No one is against human factors or supports poor human factors. Accordingly, we, in the field, have a different task. It is not to convince people of the importance of human factors, but to define what human factors are and dig out some of the many unspoken and deeply rooted misconceptions. I believe that there are many users, engineers, and designers who (privately, perhaps subconsciously) hold such views. The misconceptions are largely unspoken, and reflect more a set of estblished attitudes.

In one way or another, these misconceptions suggest that true human engineering is not easy. They also suggest that there are some common themes and thickets that are true for most users most of the time. There is a logic to user behavior. Professional programmers and designers can capture this logic to produce software that allows a user to get on with practical work easily. This is the kind of behavior we want to optimize, a kind of human engineering for Charlie and his work.

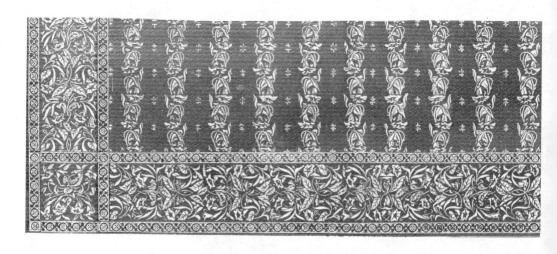

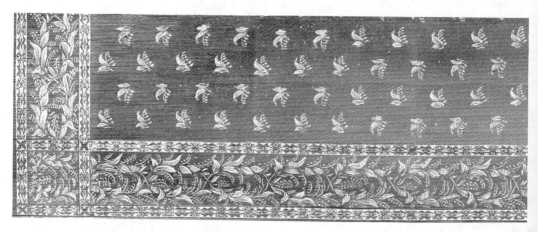

8

Three Design Tactics from Human Factors

Too often a project takes on its own kind of mystique. Its course cannot be altered; its creators are offended by suggestions, however minor. A kind of inertia sets in. Why is this?

The reason might well be simple—no one outside the inner circle of the project could possibly understand the design. Anyone asking a difficult question would get a glowing response that any reservations would be resolved successfully. A paradox presents itself. The one who can offer a critique is not privy to enough information. He or she goes quietly away, leaving the inner circle just about where it was—without the value of critique.

Human factors specialists have been saying that designers should "write the user manual first." This is an issue that brings a strong "hear, hear" from proponents. But, in practice, the idea is usually abandoned.

Human factors specialists recommend something called "user testing" or "iterative design." The designers may tell you they do that all the time, but, much more often than not, little user testing is done.

And, what does a good iterative language or menu look like? How can we avoid strange punctuation and promote simplicity?

The three design tactics, discussed below, are easily misunderstood. When well practiced, however, they have much to offer the practicing software professional.

Note: The work of John Gould et al. on the 1984 Olympic Message System is highly recommended for this chapter. This work describes the use of many design principles that put the user first.

Writing the User Manual First

The goal itself is simple: Write the complete user manual first. "First" means first, that is, before coding. "Complete" means with appendices and error messages, when appropriate. This is called a preliminary or developmental user manual.

There are several practical questions that have to be answered:

Can it be done?
Will it slow the schedule?
Will changes make the effort useless?
Is it really that important?
Is it a task for software engineers?
Are software engineers qualified to do it?
Doesn't the user want to see the system, not a manual?

These issues deserve elaboration.

The view that the user manual cannot be written before implementation is often a symptom of other problems. Perhaps the implementors have doubts about the system or, as currently conceived, perhaps the system is so unclear that it is unreasonable to describe its behavior on paper. These are symptoms of a project without any defined lifecycle. There are cases in which research and development are needed before a final design is fully conceived. This work, and often prototypes, must be completed before any reasonable manual can be written. Nonetheless, if it is possible to write the code, it is certainly possible to write the manual.

Taking the time to document a system of some complexity may require considerable effort. But will it slow the project's schedule? On the contrary, on balance, writing the user manual first usually *speeds* the project. In later stages, it provides a succinct statement of the system to implementors. It helps them develop the software and serves as a convenient way of getting external feedback on the design itself.

The user manual in this sense is developmental. One considers it to be a final statement of the user interface and taken seriously as such. Later, as development proceeds, changes are incorporated. Thus, the manual provides a forum for stating changes and making only those changes that will enhance the general design rather than add more and more sideline features. But the simple fact of having this document early in development is a bonus to all. It is reasonable to test some of the ideas in the user manual before embarking on the final implementation. Moreover, writing the manual early may take effort, but it will tend to promote a system of higher quality.

All users want the system to be delivered; that is natural. But having the manual early can have a clear and positive impact on potential users. Programmers can see the system in some form before the final design is accepted for development. The manual can be given outside to representatives or consultants for their evaluation. The user requirements document, normally a document with many generalities, has its fulfillment in terms of a concrete manual. "Surprises" can be avoided. If the design is not appropriate for some reason, it is much easier to revise the *manual* at this stage than to revise the *system* at a later stage. Most users when given the chance to see a user's manual first will seize the opportunity.

There is a feeling that documentation (and manuals, in particular) is a boring part of the software engineering process. Software engineering teams may feel unqualified to bring the manual to fruition. On the other hand, writing the user manual early is more beneficial than writing it at the end. Having it in hand gives excitement to the project and a focus for future development.

If a team feels unqualified to write the user manual or is under too much pressure, there are several alternatives. We can put together *something* in print, even if it's not the best. Or we can get assistance by bringing in someone qualified to organize what exists into printed form. If possible, we should try to have a technical person write it.

One must be careful to avoid cases where help is a net negative. One must also watch out for the "I'm not a good writer" excuse. A good manual requires good thinking and good organization. These are more important than good "writing." The one who is not a "good writer" may be someone who has never tried or just lacks confidence.

PANEL
A Developmental User Manual as a Design Tactic

- Prevents mistakes
- Fosters better design
- Clears up vague ideas
- Focus for development
- Easy to get sensible product review
- Helpful to implementors

Finally, writing the user manual first is another statement of belief in the top-down development process, where the top is the user. Writing the user manual first takes the smokescreen off the project, makes it visible, and makes it sensible. It is, if you will, a top-down design device at the highest level.

User Testing

We now discuss a design technique called "user testing" or "iterative design" or "iterative testing." User testing is not a research technique but a design technique. It can be (but need not always be) expensive in time and money to apply.

What is user testing? This is a typical pattern.

1. Take a prototype of a proposed system.
2. Develop a short task for the system.
3. Recruit some representative users.
4. Observe the users performing the task on the prototype.
5. Based on these observations, make recommendations for design changes.
6. Repeat this process as seems appropriate until an acceptable design is obtained.

Another view of this process is given in Figure 8.1.

Normally, the item to be tested is a prototype of a system. The item can be a document, such as a user's guide or an installation procedures manual. In all cases the item to be tested is a piece of work. It is a piece of work that portends an actual product. The work may be in its very preliminary stages or close to a completed design.

We may need to build only a facade imitating a proposed design. For example, if we are testing a proposed filing system, it is not necessary that the files be maintained. They may not even exist, as long as the user has the illusion that they do. The prototype also may be skeletal, a preliminary piece of software that embodies some new thinking.

The subjects should be representative of the population of users who will ultimately buy or use the product. If one is testing a set of labels for a keyboard for an accounting system, those testing the product should be representative of the accounting community. It is not necessary to recruit them in any formal way, as long as they are potential users of the system at hand. A caveat is in order: using one's friends or professional peers as subjects usually produces an unnecessary bias in the results of the testing.

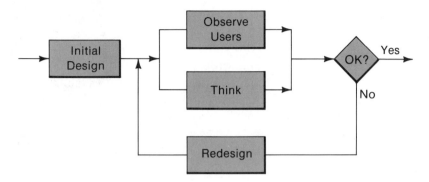

Figure 8.1 User testing

The testing should be carried out using a short, fixed task. This is a powerful notion, giving one a benchmark to know if the design is actually improving. While the task does not have to be picked at the outset and frozen during the entire design cycle, centering one's attention on a task eliminates a number of spurious effects. The task might be simply creating and sending a message on an electronic mail system. For testing a user's guide, the task might be simply reading the guide until one can enter and run a simple three-line program. The objective is: fix one or more benchmark tasks that can be used during the evaluation. These are the measures of progress.

The issue of observing subjects is complex. One way is simply to watch the subject performing a task. Unfortunately, when a user gets stuck on a particular operation, it is all too easy to intervene and lose sight of the difficulties that occur when problems arise. It is difficult not to influence behavior. Sitting quietly in a corner or using a third party to observe is perhaps more useful.

There are other ways to observe behavior and all require a greater investment beforehand. One can put monitors in the software to capture keystrokes and the times at which they occurred. This gives a running log of the session and is available for later inspection. This approach, while certainly more precise, requires reviewing the listings in order to gather meaningful observations. When screen interaction is involved, listings tend to fall short of the mark.

Enhancing the testing further, one can make video recordings of the subjects, their comments, and the contents of the screen. This is a potent technique. The anguish and difficulty the subjects face is then recorded for all to see. One can make excerpts to show designers exactly where the subjects ran into trouble. In the work of [Good, et al., 1984], dramatic improvements in the software were achieved after making video recordings of subjects using an electronic mail system. The system was improved after each series of subjects. When the software reached its final state, subjects were able to do significantly more work with significantly more satisfaction. Granted, using video tapes requires a deep commitment to the idea of user testing; but they can make differences that are so striking that it may even turn a mediocre product into an excellent one.

User testing does not always involve additional costs. If misguided ideas are discovered in the beginning, generous savings can be realized to make the time and effort for user testing pale in comparison. There are endless arguments about one design alternative versus another alternative and about investing a great deal of energy and development effort in an idea that, when it comes to the users, just doesn't work. Stopping these things early is a clear saving.

When is the appropriate time to do user testing? The greatest payoff comes from doing it in the early design stages. An early test of possible and promising ideas will always prove beneficial. True, this can be uncomfortable if the software is in no reasonable state to give any semblance of performance. One may have to create rather haphazardly produced mockups. But it is only at the beginning where one can effectively spot and test basic design philosophies. This involves not only the larger design issues, such as using menus or commands, but also the lesser problems, such as the format for screen windows, the style of messages, the general syntax that the user must obey, the methods of file handling, and so forth. Certain of these ideas will emerge as proven; others may be questionable. Designers have less of a commitment to a given idea early on and more readily turn to ideas that are proven with users.

In the later stages of development, user testing is more refined. One may spot diagnostic messages that are unclear or a particular command style that is awkward and generally not understood. This kind of pruning is similar to the debugging of a piece of software. Improvements and corrections can be made in the user's favor. Unfortunately, when user testing is only employed at the end of a project, the result may be the discovery of a catastrophe.

Two points mentioned previously are worth greater emphasis. First, if this approach is taken seriously, the gains are more likely to be beneficial than not. Second, the earlier one performs user testing the better. Ideally user testing should be a design method employed throughout the development cycle. Overusing the cliche, "the early bird catches the worm," the late worm may be too late.

PANEL
User Testing as a Design Tactic

- Prevents mistakes
- Exposes bottlenecks
- Promotes new thinking
- Resolves competing designs

- Helps eliminate revised releases
- Helps appreciate the true user
- Serves as a tuning device
- Gives measurable criteria for success

Even when designers are aware of it, user testing is seldom employed. Probably the greatest argument against it is that time becomes too precious in development. There is no software product project that is not under tight time constraints, that is, not subject to slippages in schedules and cost overruns. This makes any new idea appear to take more time than necessary. The only effective antidote may be one's next project, not the present one. Some development groups seem to defy all the odds and take all the risks.

Another argument against user testing is that it may not be worth it. After all, the designers' sensibilities are usually considered sacred. The users are in no position to define systems, so why bother to involve the user at all? First of all, with user testing, the users do *not* do the design. But they do have certain kinds of behavior, certain expectations, and certain predispositions that we do not realize. The hypothesis is that, whatever the user's logic, it can be captured by observation, and then translated by the designers into effective solutions.

Finally, there is a subtle argument against user testing that is seldom visible. User testing, like writing the user manual first, can be too revealing for the designers. Watching subjects suffer with a system that is supposedly easy to use can be a bit too much for some people. But, when done well, user testing does not result in a few computer printouts from which one can extract some simple improvements. Rather, it is a potent excursion into the live operation of a planned system. The results can be startling. Rubenstein and Hersh [1984] summed it up this way—you build it, you test it.

Note: My inspiration for user testing comes from John Whiteside [see Good et al., 1984]. This work by John Gould and others on the 1984 Olympic message system demonstrates the use of this technique in its fullest measure.

A Familiar Notation for Users

Interactive systems are now commonplace. At a minimal level, the user may be prompted for data:

```
System: Enter number of items:
User:    14
System: Specify Voltage Range:
User:    1.5;3.5
```

The user may be asked to answer a question,

```
System: Do you wish to preserve changes?
User:    Y
```

At a higher level of interaction, the user may respond to a simple one-line menu such as

```
System: N REORDER(R) EDIT(E) RUN(N) FILE(F) MERGE(M)  EXIT(X)
```

or more typically, a menu like

```
System: 1. ELECTRONIC MAIL
        2. REDO FILES
        3. WORD PROCESSING
        4. CALCULATE
        5. DRAWING
        6. GAME PLAYING
        7. MORE CHOICES
User:    3
```

In both cases, the user has to formulate some kind of response. At an even higher level of control, the user may issue commands directly:

```
System: . . .
User:    save
System: **FILE REPORT2 SAVED
User:    print REPORT2.TEXT; SPACING=2
```

Designers of interactive software must answer questions like these:

How should prompts be written?

Should the entries in a menu look like mini-commands?

What command names should we use? Should we use verb-object or object-verb?

Should a positional notation be used for arguments?

Should we allow for synonyms?

Here are a few principles which, although only a part of the problem, may assist software engineers in understanding this problem.

The issue here is what the user types to initiate an action; included are conventional commands, selection from a menu, responses to prompts; excluded are special-purpose keys, form-fill-ins, and pointing devices (such as a mouse). Another way of making this distinction is that typing actions are included, but forms of direct manipulation are not. Thus, typed utterances can be considered as a kind of "language." The other forms of input are viewed as buttons used to operate a mechanical device.

One principle is: Consider using spoken language as a model for syntax. Consider the following top-level menu, which might occur in a general-purpose system:

```
Use Electronic Mail
Use File Manager
Use Word Processing
Use Calculator
Use Drawing Functions
Use Video Games
See More Choices
```

This is a syntax in the normal sense in that there is a simple grammar underlying the set of selections. It is a verb followed by its object. Together the verb and object constitute a verb phrase. All of these phrases might be used in *spoken* communication to suggest the selection. Notice the special phrase, "See More Choices." This verb phrase is deliberately different from the rest because it suggests a continuation of the top-level menu.

Selection of a given item in a menu is often achieved by numbering or by using a pointing device. In a system that has a parallel command-menu strategy, the user can also type the selected entry. If we follow the first-letter abbreviation rule (to be discussed in more detail later), the user can type any one of the following:

```
UEM
UFM
UWP
UC
UDF
UVG
SMC
```

Notice that with such a simple abbreviation rule it may, in fact, be just as quick to type the abbreviated forms as to view and select a given number or to move a pointing device to the selected entry. In an example like this, I have no particular objection to eliminating the word "use." But, for consistency, I recommend a stricter syntax for the noun phrases.

We must also make sure that the user draws the (correct) inference and that is that the grammar is a highly restricted one without the suggested power of natural language. Here, it is important to draw upon uniform strategies of syntax. For example, it is common for the user to tell the system that certain things ought to be remembered and then used in subsequent dialogues. Drawing a syntax from [Singer et al., 1981], one might adopt a strategy such as

```
ASSUME WILD CARD    SYMBOL IS "?"
ASSUME ELLIPSIS     SYMBOL IS "..."
ASSUME NEW PAGE     SYMBOL IS "-*-"
ASSUME RIGHT MARGIN SYMBOL IS "/"
ASSUME DIGIT        SYMBOL IS "d"
```

Here one imagines the user is coining special symbols for use in a general-purpose editing system. Now, with the first-letter abbreviation rule, these commands would become

```
AWCSI "?"
AESI  "..."
ANRSI "-*-"
ARMSI "/"
ADSI  "d"
```

Notice there is good reason to use the conventional double-quote character as a means of specifying literal strings.

In another environment, for example, a drawing package, one might adopt a strategy such as,

```
SET SCREEN INTENSITY TO  1  2  3  4  5
SET GRID TO              ON  OFF
SET MENU PROMPTING TO    ON  OFF
SET LINE THICKNESS TO    THIN  MEDIUM  HEAVY
SET LABEL TO             "xxxxx"
SET DRAWING MODE TO      MANUAL  AUTOMATIC
SET MESSAGE MODE TO      TERSE  NORMAL
```

In this little example, the system might simultaneously display the default options that apply until the user requests a change. These examples could be collectively shown in response to a command like

```
CHANGE SETTINGS
```

The principle of notations inspired by a spoken language can take many forms. For example, in a line-numbered environment, we may have utterances like

```
SAVE LINES   30 TO 50
COPY LINES   30 TO 50
MOVE LINES   30 TO 50
DELETE LINES 30 TO 50
```

Again notice the consistency. Other miscellaneous forms might be

```
SET FONT OPTIONS          -- invoke a fill-in form
CHANGE DIRECTORY TO SYSTEM -- revert to systems directory
CHANGE TAB 10 TO 15       -- tab adjustment
FIND "Jones"              -- string search
SET TABS AT 10,20,40      -- three tabs
DISPLAY DATE              -- show date on screen
INSERT OPTIONAL HYPHEN    -- at cursor position
NEXT PAGE                 -- display next page
NEXT SUBROUTINE           -- display next subroutine
```

In systems with a small interface, one can get by with forms that are considerably terser. In some cases, one might even get by with simple one-line menus, for example,

```
Delete  Copy  Move  Enlarge  Reduce
```

or

```
START  FINISH  RESUME
```

As always, consistency is central.
   Notice that simple dialogues like

```
System: Enter file name:
User:    RPT1
System: Save changes?
User:    Y
```

are compatible with our principles. The spoken response is precisely what is expected. Notice also that

```
System: Enter two voltage:
User:    1.4;3.4
```

is not compatible, since the semi-colon is not a common separator of two values.

With the one-line menu given earlier

```
REORDER(R)  EDIT(E)  RUN(N)  FILE(F)  MERGE(M)  EXIT(X)
```

the menu could be redone as follows:

```
ORDER  EDIT  RUN  FILE  MERGE  QUIT
```

where the first-letter abbreviation holds, even at the expense of a possible awkward word, ORDER.

For the voltage example, I suggest a comma or a blank as a separator.

System: Enter two voltages:
User: 1.4, 3.4
User: 1.4 3.4

For a voltage range, I suggest one of

System: Specify voltage range:
User: 1.5 - 3.5
User: 1.5 .. 3.5
User: 1.5 ... 3.5

This discussion has suggested that it is possible to get by with a first-letter abbreviation rule; that is, all system words (keywords) can be abbreviated by their first letter. Thus, instead of typing

```
INSERT PAGE BREAK
```

the user can type I P B. With some care, the need for medial spaces can also be eliminated, allowing the user to type IPB.

This is not a special sequence of letters that the user must remember—not at all. The user can *think* the phrase,

```
INSERT PAGE BREAK
```

and type IPB/ Thus, the user need only remember the specific phrase for the abbreviation to be deduced.

To get this kind of rule, one must have a certain regularity to the grammar. Even though the same keyword is used in several commands, it is only necessary that the complete letter sequences be unique.

Because only the letter sequences must be unique, the designer has considerable flexibility. Utterances can be created over and over again, as long as the full sequence does not clash with previous utterances. For instance, we would have a clash between the commands

```
SEND DATA TO user-id
SET DIRECTORY TO directory-name
```

In these cases one must adopt slightly different wording to avoid ambiguity. Obviously one must be careful to limit the number of single-word commands, because these clash immediately. Probably five or ten single-word commands would be the limit. This seems a small price to pay for the value of a sound general rule.

In short, I offer these three broad principles:

1. Spoken conversation is a good model for the design of notations.
2. Consistency is a goal for any notation.
3. A uniform first-letter abbreviation rule is a powerful adjunct to easy input.

I know the reader may not fully see the point behind this, but such a scheme can open doors.

Note: The principles stated previously stem from an early work by Singer [see Singer et al., 1980]. They have been inspired mainly by a good deal of thinking about the nature of interactive systems and user input notations. However, there is some strong experimental support for this view. In an early study [Ledgard et al., 1980], an experiment was run comparing a text editor drawn from commercial literature and a semantically equivalent editor in which only the user input notation was changed along the lines given here. This study showed significant performance gains even though only the syntax of the user interface was changed.

In another study [Good et al., 1984], users were asked to generate spontaneous commands during the use of an electronic mail facility. As more users were tested with spontaneous commands, the grammar was modified to accommodate a greater number of input data. A final grammar that was comfortable to users emerged. This grammar was not at all like those of conventional systems but more of the form of pigeon English, heavily based on constructs taken from spoken conversation. Here, again, when the input notation was suitably modified, large performance gains were made.

As for the abbreviation rule, it is hard to find any data conflicting with the ease of use of simply using the first letter.

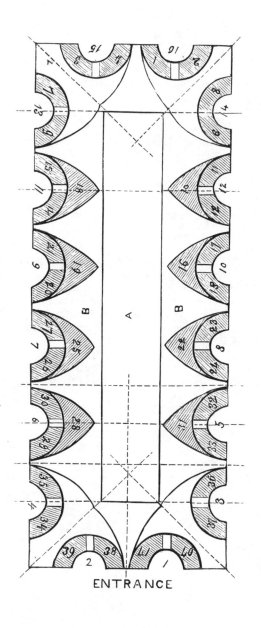

ENTRANCE

9

On Packages
and
Software Decomposition

The idea of partitioning software into parts has been with us as long as programming. Traditionally, decomposition was handled through subprograms (procedures and functions). Subprograms embody the idea of a complex action that can be summarized in terms of a simple interface to the outside world. That is, it accepts some input, may update some values, and produce some output. Ideally, all inputs, updates, and output are itemized in the subprogram header.

Unfortunately the world of programming has generally allowed the idea of a subprogram to be diverted from its simple conception. One diversion is the use of global variables. This means that the abstraction from the outside world must be deduced from knowledge of the code itself. A second diversion occurs when a procedure performs several kinds of operations at once. A subprogram should have one entry, one exit, and, importantly, one purpose [see Myers 1978].

The concept of a subprogram, however, does not always capture many decomposition problems in software. This has given rise to various concepts in contemporary programming, for example, "abstract" data types, tables, "knowledge-based" languages. The issue here is the concept of "packages." The idea of a package is itself probably quite old but owes much of its clarity to the design of the Ada facility for package declarations and package bodies, as well as the "module" concept in Modula-2 [Wirth 1983]. The concept, however well-embodied in Ada or Modula-2, is language independent. It is the idea of the package that counts. The package concept is a useful programming strategy, even though expressing it is difficult in some languages.

In a case study by [Gannon et al. 1986], it was reported that a small team of programmers did not make effective use of packages, even though the software was written in Ada. The study (only one example) suggests that the use of packages is not obvious. It takes time, training, and effort before the package concept becomes a natural and powerful design strategy.

Here we consider some broad ideas about packages. In Volume II of this two-volume work we discuss some examples.

The Concept of a Package

A package is a collection of information. In a well-designed package, the information is related to a single purpose and that purpose has a restricted meaning related to the problem being solved. The last point deserves closer scrutiny—more later.

A package defines a service that is made available to other portions of a program. In a similar vein, a subprogram also defines a service—in particular, an action or a mapping from input to output. The service provided by a package, however, is more general.

Consider the following procedure heading:

```
procedure GET_INTEGER ({ in}  PROMPT_MSG: STRING;
                               MINVAL,
                               MAXVAL: INTEGER;
                       {out} var RESULT: INTEGER);
```

This heading describes the service offered by a subprogram. In particular, the procedure GET_INTEGER takes three input values: a message for prompting the user for an input, the minimum allowed value of the input, and the maximum allowed value. It returns the value given by the user after doing the necessary checking and reprompting to guarantee that an acceptable input value is entered. The body of the procedure GET_INTEGER may or may not be complex, depending upon the kind of checking provided.

From the caller's point of view the effect of the procedure can be abstracted in terms of its input and output. This is the service provided by the procedure. It is in this sense that we say that the procedure heading

characterizes the *visible part* of the procedure. The statements and local
declarations in the procedure body describe its *implementation part.*

Next consider the following declarations:

```
type CONFIRMATION = (YES, NO);

procedure GET_INTEGER ({in}  PROMPT_MSG: STRING;
                              MINVAL,
                              MAXVAL: INTEGER;
                       {out} var RESULT: INTEGER);

procedure GET_REAL     ({using} PROMPT_MSG: STRING;
                                MINVAL,
                                MAXVAL: REAL;
                        {giving} var RESULT: REAL);

procedure GET_GO_AHEAD ({using}  PROMPT_MSG: STRING;
                         {giving} var RESPONSE:  CONFIRMATION);
```

Here we have a type and three procedure headings. This is the kind of service
that a package might perform. In particular, there are three procedures for
obtaining input values from the user as well as a new type introduced to
handle yes-no responses to questions. Implementing this service may require
additional routines, for checking input values, or handling spurious input.
But, again, from the caller's point of view, as long as the service is
implemented in some reasonable way, the package can be abstracted in these
simple terms.

To talk about packages, it is helpful to adopt a little syntax. Consider the
following sketch:

```
package SAMPLE;
    { -- visible part }
    constant, type, and variable declarations
    subprogram headers
end;

package body SAMPLE;
    { -- implementation part }
    local constants, types, and variables
    supporting subprograms
    definition of visible subprograms
end;
```

The service offered by a package is expressed as its visible part. This may
contain the declaration of constants, types, variables, procedures, and
functions. The visible subprograms are denoted by giving their headers only.

The body of the package describes the computations needed to complete the service offered by the visible part. In particular, the body may contain the declaration of local constants, variables, and types. It may also contain subprograms needed in a supporting role. Finally, the visible subprograms, those whose headers are listed in the visible part, are fully defined.

The program at the end of this work makes use of this notation. Each item listed in the visible part is automatically visible in the corresponding implementation part. Any other program unit that makes use of the package must include an *import* or *inherit* clause in its header, for example:

```
inherit SAMPLE;
```

All items listed in the visible part become visible in the inheriting unit. Complexities, such as name conflicts and package initialization, need not concern us in this work.

Packages as a Design Notation

A programming team needs to divide work in a coherent way. Even a programmer working alone needs to characterize the task at hand in some effective way. It is fine for Fred to say, "I'll just get the I/O routines going", but such statements can turn into platitudes. Packages, on the other hand, are a notation for characterizing units of work. They can serve a vital role, turning good intentions into something that can be seen and understood—the visible part of the package itself.

The challenge is—*What is a reasonable partition of the work?* The typical programming task has many parts. The parts are interrelated in subtle ways. The partitioning of the work should make intrusion from other packages as minimal as possible.

Imagine a program to read and update a small inventory of parts. The user of the program may wish to find out how many ABC Widgets are in stock or, say, record a new shipment of ABC Widgets. Such a program can be organized in endless ways. Some of the questions that must be answered are:

Should the description of parts be in the same package as the description of the inventory file?

Should command syntax be part of the package for input of data?

Should the user input and output be combined into a single package?

Should file operations be part of the same package that describes the file contents?

Should there be a package of general-purpose routines?

Should the printing of messages be separated from user output?

Should we have many packages or just a few?

None of these issues is necessarily easy to resolve.

One possible decomposition could run as follows:

MAIN   The top-level routines.

PARTS_INFO   All about the data kept on parts.

COMMANDS   All about the commands issued by the program user.

USER_IO   All about the messages and screen interface seen by the user.

INVENTORY   All about the permanent inventory file.

Here the program is divided into a main routine and four packages. Such a decomposition seems reasonable, but without further information about the problem one must be careful not to make much of a commitment.

A particular decomposition is of little value until it is spelled out in detail. For packages, this means putting the visible part of the package in writing. This is a hard step to make, but its value is considerable. The actual decomposition must be forced out into the open.

For the package PARTS_INFO mentioned previously, the visible part of the package may come out to be something like

```
package PARTS_INFO:
   const
      MAX_NAME_LENGTH = 20;
      CODE_LENGTH     =  3;

   type
      PART_NAME = array [1..MAX_NAME_LENGTH] of CHAR;
      PART_CODE = array [1..CODE_LENGTH] of CHAR;

   PART_NAME_INFO =
         record
            FULL: PART_NAME;
            CODE: PART_CODE;
         end;

   ORDER_STATUS = (NONE, PENDING, ON_ORDER, SHIPPED);
   . . .
   end;
```

Here, protocols are spelled out; decisions are made. A commitment is made to the overall problem solution.

As a design notation, the package concept can be enhanced in various ways. At an informal level, one might use a kind of pseudo-language for the visible part:

```
package SCREEN_HANDLER;

    -- constants for fixed fields
    -- types for variable length data
    -- type NEW_ENTRY = record...end;

    task CONTROL_CMD
        entry POST_DATA (parameters);
        entry UPDATE_STATUS (parameters);
        ...
        entry CLEAR_ALL;
    end;
end;
```

Even more potently, one can spell out the design in detail using a specific computer language. For instance, using an example derived from [Harbison and Steele, 1984], one could define a package-like facility using C. This gives something like:

```
package STACK
    #define NULL_ELEM
    ...
    typedef int element_type;
    ...
    typedef struct {
        element_type *BASE;
        element_type *END;
        element_type *NEXT;
    } *stack_info;
    ...
    extern void PUSH ();
        /* PUSH (stack_name, element) */
end.
```

Using Modula-2 or Ada directly as a design notation is especially powerful. In these languages, the notation for packages is built in and the package concept is a natural one for a design notation.

Problem Basis

It is easy to decompose a system into parts that make more sense in terms of the syntax of the language or a given set of implementation techniques. The

challenge is to decompose the system in *problem-oriented* terms.
Consider the following:

A collection of commonly used types, constants, and procedures.
A set of utility routines.
A collection of parsing algorithms.
The collection of global arrays and structures.
All constants needed in a physics program.

As packages, these usually present difficulties. For example, consider a package specifying all the constants in a program related to a physics problem. Such a package would define the maximum length of an input line, the maximum depth of a stack, the names for the maximum values of physical properties, the names for conversion factors, and so on. Such a collection makes little sense in problem-oriented terms because it is based on the syntactic unit of a constant declaration.

Similarly, a collection of utility routines might define functions for converting between various units of measure, low-level input-output procedures, procedures to edit data, procedures to print in a given format, and so on. Such a collection is organized simply on the basis that the routines are frequently used.

A tougher issue is a collection of procedures and types needed to interface with low-level hardware. If these are grouped together only because the routines interface with low-level devices (not because they have a common use), clarity is sacrificed.

Consider instead the following:

- A collection of metric conversion factors.
- A definition of part numbers and their corresponding part names.
- A set of routines for managing cursor movement.
- The definition of a linked list and the allowed operations on the lists.
- The constants, types, and procedures for managing the user interface.
- A set of routines for compressing files.
- The routines for prompting and getting back answers in a dialogue.

Each of these suggests a well-defined collection of information. They capture a state of knowledge. They express the meaning of a given concept. Although the line is not usually simple, they are all potentially good packages.

One good way to think about packages is as a collection of items pertinent to a given state of knowledge. For instance, consider

- The constants, types, and procedures needed to embody the idea of shuffling and dealing cards in a game playing program.

This description presents a solid view in problem-oriented terms. We can easily relate to such a package. Similarly, consider

- The collection of types and routines needed for effective layout of information on the screen.

With the right problem, this too can be a wise choice for a package.

Packages can give a programming team greater latitude in specifying units of work. Moreover, they can capture design and decomposition issues in meaningful terms. When supplemented with notations for types, procedure headers, tasks, and so forth, packages can become a powerful design notation.

10

Empirical
Methods

In recent years, there has been interest in the human factors of programming and computer systems and, in particular, in empirical studies. Generally, empirical work falls into two broad categories:

1. *Experiments.* In its pure form, an experiment is quite simple. It is an attempt to show that some theory X is superior to some theory Y.
2. *Gathering data.* Here the objective is more diffuse. Code listings, on-line terminal usage, or user reactions are examined to discover what people actually do. The purpose here is to discover relevant issues.

An experiment begins with a hypothesis—for example, "design diagrams are easier to read than pseudo code" or "programmers prefer to use method A over method B." This kind of work is useful in setting principles, narrow or board, for software development. Data gathering, a long-respected technique in the scientific community, is common to computer systems. Data can give us insight into which features of a system are little used, where trouble spots lie, and where programmers devote their energies.

There is a third category that falls under empirical work. This is

3. *User testing.* Here, proposed designs of actual systems are submitted to users. The behavior of the user is monitored to discover flaws in the design.

This is the subject of another chapter.

The simple categorization just made is not always accurate. For example, experiments are run without any clear hypothesis of what to expect. The experiment may just compare two program constructs to see which turns out to be superior, if one does at all. The best experiments have a clear hypothesis at the outset.

The objective in this chapter is to relate, in a broad sense, experimental work in programming to some of the topics discussed in this book. I have deliberately refrained from citing experimental work, especially in the examples on programming practice of Volume II. My belief is that this area needs clarification. To do this, we now consider some hypothetical experiments. None of these experiments, to my knowledge, has been carried out in the form presented here.

In what follows, we are not particularly concerned with detailed statistical matters, for example, sample size, counterbalancing, and scoring methods. Our interest is only in the general experimental design and sizable gross effects.

Note: There is a fine collection of experimental works in a lengthy volume entitled *Human Factors in Software Development,* edited by Bill Curtis [see Curtis, 1981 and its update, Curtis, 1986]. These volumes are noteworthy since almost all of the experimental work relates in some way to programming. Two other good sources are the January 1986 *Communications of the ACM* [see Davis, 1986] and the July 1986 *Communications of the ACM* [see Ledgard, 1986].

A Program Layout Experiment

The first experiment could have come straight from a textbook. We wish to determine the effect of program layout upon program comprehension. The experiment is roughly as follows:

1. Two one-page program listings are prepared. They are identical except for their layout and are given here as Figures 10.1a and 10.1b.
2. The first listing follows an uninspired style. In particular, loops are not indented and no particular concern is given to its layout.
3. The second listing employs conventional layout techniques advocated by structured programming proponents. In particular, the bodies of if statements and loops are indented. Blank lines are inserted at strategic places. Alignment is used where customary.

4. Twenty subjects are recruited from a graduate course in software engineering. Ten subjects use listing 10.1a; the other ten listing 10.1b.
5. In order to measure comprehension, a number of questions are asked about the program. Typical of these questions are:
   a. What will the final value of CMD.STRING_LEN be for the header "Final Report"?
   b. Will the empty header "" set CMD.NAME to ERROR?
   c. Must a header have both an opening and closing quotation mark?
6. The subjects are given a period of time, say 5 or 10 minutes, to answer the questions, and the results are scored.

What will happen?

Already, the experiment has potential pitfalls. Does the procedure have proper mnemonic names? If the procedure does have exceptionally clear names, perhaps the given code excerpt will speak for itself without regard to indentation. How important is program layout in these examples? The examples may be short enough that layout will not be an important issue in comprehension. What length of time should the subjects have to answer the questions? The questions may be easy enough that most of the subjects will answer most of the questions consistently, independent of the layout. All of these factors tend to produce a null result, i.e., an indication that the hypothesis being tested (that program layout is important) fails to show a significant effect.

In the extreme, one could remove every blank line and extra blank space and simply give the code as a string of characters. Imagine trying to read the procedure were it to fit on 10 or 12 lines. Obviously, this alternative would produce a dramatic effect and indicate that program layout was certainly significant.

The general problem raised is the following—Experimental "noise" may be greater than the effect being measured. Program layout *is* important, but the proposed experiment may not show it.

How would one empirically show the importance of program layout? Some suggestions are as follows:

Eliminate mnemonic names. Simply give all variables a single-letter name; then produce the two listings, one spaced and one not spaced. This might (although perhaps not) have a significant effect.

Use a section of code that is much longer than the one given here and for which program layout is a major issue in its readability.

Figure 10.1
Programs for Layout Experiment

a. *Lack of Program Layout*

```
procedure PARSE_HEADER (LINE: LINE_INFO; START_POS: INTEGER;
     var CMD:  COMMAND_INFO);
{ This procedure analyzes the header for a HEADER
  command. If the header is invalid, CMD.NAME is set to ERROR.
  Otherwise the header is assigned to CMD.STRING_ARG. }
  const QUOTE_MARK = '"';

  var POSITION: INTEGER;
  LENGTH:   INTEGER;

begin
    if LINE.IMAGE[START_POS] = QUOTE_MARK then
    begin
    POSITION := START_POS + 1; LENGTH := 0;
    while (LINE.IMAGE[POSITION] <> QUOTE_MARK)
    and (POSITION < LINE.WIDTH) do
    begin
    LENGTH := LENGTH + 1;
    CMD.STRING_ARG[LENGTH] := LINE.IMAGE[POSITION];
    POSITION := POSITION + 1
    end
    end;

    if (LINE.IMAGE[START_POS] <> QUOTE_MARK)
    or (LINE.IMAGE[POSITION] <> QUOTE_MARK)
    then begin
    CMD.NAME := ERROR;
    CMD.STRING_LEN := 0 end
    else CMD.STRING_LEN := LENGTH
end;
```

Figure 10.1 (continued)

b. *Good Program Layout*

```
procedure PARSE_HEADER (LINE:      LINE_INFO;
                        START_POS: INTEGER;
                        var CMD:   COMMAND_INFO);

{ -- This procedure analyzes the header for a HEADER command.
  -- If the header is invalid, CMD.NAME is set to ERROR.
  -- Otherwise the header is assigned to CMD.STRING_ARG. }

   const
      QUOTE_MARK = '"';

   var
      POSITION: INTEGER;
      LENGTH:   INTEGER;

begin
   if LINE.IMAGE[START_POS] = QUOTE_MARK then begin
      POSITION := START_POS + 1;
      LENGTH    := 0;

      while (LINE.IMAGE[POSITION] <> QUOTE_MARK)
      and (POSITION < LINE.WIDTH) do begin
         LENGTH := LENGTH + 1;
         CMD.STRING_ARG[LENGTH] := LINE.IMAGE[POSITION];
         POSITION := POSITION + 1
      end
   end;

   if (LINE.IMAGE[START_POS] <> QUOTE_MARK)
   or (LINE.IMAGE[POSITION]  <> QUOTE_MARK)
   then
      begin
         CMD.NAME := ERROR;
         CMD.STRING_LEN := 0
      end
   else
      CMD.STRING_LEN := LENGTH
end;
```

Consider a larger program, say, 50 pages. Remove all page breaks and blank lines. Now make the task a series of simple lookups; for example,

find procedure MARK_GRAPH
find the declaration of COORD
find the assignment of 12 to GRID_POS
...

without regard to comprehension. This is a very pointed experiment, centering only on the idea of whether page breaks and blank lines help.

These kinds of experiments, I believe, would have a greater chance of succeeding.

A Naming Experiment

Now let us consider another experiment, one on naming. Again, we have two versions of a program. Our new experiment will run as follows:

1. Two listings are prepared; one with short names and one with longer, more suggestive names. These are given in Figure 10.2.
2. Twenty subjects are again recruited; ten are given one version and ten the other. A list of questions about the code is compiled, for example:
   a. What value will the header "Final Report" give for a length?
   b. Will the empty header "" set the command name status to ERROR?
   c. Must a header have both an opening and closing quotation mark?
3. The subjects are given a limited period of time to answer the questions, and the results are scored. The time is short enough that most subjects will not be able to finish.

What will happen?

Here the experiment has been deliberately contrived so that the average programmer will not be able to complete all of the questions. In some experiments, this is a fine idea. It tests people's first response to the code, which is probably more indicative of how the code speaks for itself. Given enough time, many programmers would be able to answer all of the questions accurately no matter how poorly the code is written.

However, this experiment has a different kind of problem than the program layout experiment discussed earlier. This problem is—The "better" version may not be better. Choosing proper names is a challenge. If you notice, the second version of the program, the one with the supposedly mnemonic names, is itself questionable on a naming basis. I submit that these are typical of names that an average programmer might choose without giving the matter careful thought. The names have slightly off-target suggestiveness. Unless a name is carefully chosen with due regard to possible ambiguities, the names may, in fact, be counterproductive. The names in the second version may (but not necessarily) have this problem and, again, the experiment may turn out to prove little.

An Experiment on the Use of Procedures

We now increase the difficulty index significantly. The following experiment is intended to illustrate whether the idea of one-procedure, one-purpose is a useful strategy in programming. You may say, "of course it is"; but my experience has lead me to believe that procedures with a single purpose are not exactly as common as we would like to think. Perhaps the difficulty is getting the appropriate levels of abstraction; perhaps the matter is not well understood. Nevertheless, let us assume that we wish to test whether or not this is a useful idea.

Our experiment runs as follows:

1. We prepare a 5- or 6-page program, say a program to read in a list of names and addresses and print the addresses in alphabetical order.
2. The first program is written in such a way that it consists of two large procedures and a main program. The procedures have multiple purposes in the sense that issues like:
   reading the file,
   testing for accuracy of entries,
   testing for an empty file,
   sorting,
   formatting of the output,
   and so on, are not particularly well organized.
3. The second version is organized as a short main program with five or six procedures that presumably have one purpose. This second program is longer than the first.
4. Both of the programs use mnemonic names, good program layout, careful commenting, and so forth.
5. Twenty subjects are recruited, ten with each version.
6. The subjects have a limited time to answer questions about the two programs, and the results are scored.

What will happen?

This experiment has a number of difficulties, which may or may not be important depending on how the example is actually written. For instance,

Figure 10.2
Code Excerpts for a Naming Experiment

a. *Lack of Mnemonic Names*

```
procedure PARSE (LIN:    LINE_INFO;
                 SP:     INTEGER;
                 var C:  COMMAND_INFO);

{ -- This procedure analyzes the header for a HEADER command.
  -- If the header is invalid, C.N is set to ERROR.
  -- Otherwise the header is assigned to C.SARG. }

    const
        Q = '"';

    var
        POS: INTEGER;
        L:   INTEGER;

begin
    if LIN.TXT[SP] = Q then begin
        POS := SP + 1;
        L   := 0;

        while (LIN.TXT[POS] <> Q)
        and (POS < LIN.W) do begin
            L := L + 1;
            C.SARG[L] := LIN.TXT[POS];
            POS := POS + 1
        end
    end;

    if (LIN.TXT[SP]  <> Q)
    or (LIN.TXT[POS] <> Q)
    then
        begin
            C.N := ERROR;
            C.LEN := 0
        end
    else
        C.LEN := L
end;
```

Figure 10.2 (continued)

b. *Use of Mnemonic Names*

```
procedure PARSE_HEAD (INVALUE: LINE_INFO;
                      START:    INTEGER;
                      var COM: COMMAND_INFO);

{ -- This procedure analyzes the header for a HEADER command.
  -- If the header is invalid, COM.STATUS is set to ERROR.
  -- Otherwise the header is assigned to COM.STRING_ARG. }

    const
        QUOTES = '"';

    var
        COUNT:    INTEGER;
        POSITION: INTEGER;

begin
    if INVALUE.COPY[START] = QUOTES then begin
        COUNT    := START + 1;
        POSITION := 0;

        while (INVALUE.COPY[COUNT] <> QUOTES)
        and (COUNT < INVALUE.WIDTH) do begin
            POSITION := POSITION + 1;
            COM.STRING_ARG[POSITION] := INVALUE.COPY[COUNT];
            COUNT := COUNT + 1
        end;
    end;

    if (INVALUE.COPY[START] <> QUOTES)
    or (INVALUE.COPY[COUNT] <> QUOTES)
    then
        begin
            COM.STATUS := ERROR;
            COM.LENGTH := 0
        end
    else
        COM.LENGTH := POSITION
end;
```

each version may be complex enough that it is impossible to discern any effect from the procedure decomposition. There may also be considerable experimental noise brought about by the comments, layout, naming, and the algorithms used. It is these kinds of problems that make the preparation of an experiment inherently difficult. The factors that count must be distinguished from those that do not. Getting it right may take a number of iterations in the design of the experiment itself.

But even beyond these issues, there are two problems with the experiment even as conceived in its broad sense. The first is: what does one-procedure, one-purpose truly mean? It may be possible to decompose this program into two large procedures which, in effect, have a single purpose. The purpose is defined with respect to the problem domain, and has little to do with whether the procedures are large or not. Perhaps the ideal decomposition is into two general procedures, each with a subprocedure. The principle itself is difficult to understand and even more difficult to test. It does not mean that the principle is not good and that we should not attempt to achieve it, even if imperfectly. But testing it is another matter.

A second problem is the length of the example programs. It is probably true that the issue of one-procedure, one-purpose matters most as programs get larger and larger. Just as a ten-line program may show nothing about the importance of program layout, a five- or six-page program may show nothing about one-procedure, one-purpose. The example may just be too small to measure its effect. I believe the effect of the principle is indeed dramatic, but it is on a larger scale that the effect will be obvious. In short—The principle must be clearly evident.

A Design Notation Experiment

We wish to compare the use of structured English versus diagrams in their ability to convey conditional logic. Using an example derived from [Mayer, 1976], the following experiment is developed.

1. We prepare two short handouts; one expressing the problem in structured English, the other in diagramatic form. These are given in Figure 10.3.
2. Twenty subjects are recruited; ten are given one version and ten the other. A list of questions is compiled; for example,
   a. If Ohio beats Michigan, what prizes could you win?
   b. If Indiana is the best team, could you win prize E?
   c. If you won prize B, could Ohio have beaten Michigan?

3. The subjects are given a limited period of time to answer the questions, and the results are scored.

You hear that the structured English rendering wins. This gives pause for thought. Are you surprised? Are you willing to accept the hypothesis— Structured English (i.e., pseudo-code) is superior to diagrams in conveying conditional logic. No?

We need to look closely. As reported in [Mayer, 1976], a structured English solution did *not* outperform the flow diagram. Something is wrong here.

The stated result is conceivable, but the materials may well be biased. The structured English solution is carefully conceived; the flow diagram is a bit careless in that the prizes and team pairings are not especially well ordered.

Consider, instead, the materials of Figure 10.4. Here the structured English solution is tedious, but the diagram (a decision tree) is well crafted. If the experiment were run with these alternatives, I suggest that the diagram would win hands down. In fact, this is what is reported in [Mayer, 1976] and suggested in [Vessey and Weber, 1986].

The point is this: Materials are easy to bias, even if not deliberately.

Scaling Up

One of the general difficulties with pointed, single-issue experiments, while certainly valuable, is that they seldom suggest the complex problems that programmers face when trying to understand another's program. If you had the chance to examine someone else's code (at least 50 pages) and were responsible for upgrading or correcting it, you may find yourself faced with a formidable task. It is here that things like levels of abstraction, simplicity, and naming become urgent. The problems can surround you.

Consider the following excerpt:

```
if  (STATUS_ARRAY[NUM1] = PLR_PIECE)
and (STATUS_ARRAY[NUM2] = EMPTY) then
begin
  ON_JUMP := FIND_JUMP(STATUS_ARRAY, COLOR)
  if ON_JUMP then if (LT_JUMP_TABLE[COLOR,NUM1] = NUM2)
  or (RT_JUMP_TABLE[COLOR,NUM1] = NUM2) then
  TEST_MID_SQ(NUM1,NUM2,STATUS)
  else if (LT_MOVES[COLOR,NUM1] = NUM2) or
  (RT_MOVES[COLOR,NUM1] = NUM2) then
  STATUS = OK
end;
```

Figure 10.3
Structured English versus Diagrams

a. *Structured English*

There are three games:
   1. MICHIGAN versus INDIANA
   2. MICHIGAN versus OHIO
   3. INDIANA versus OHIO

">" means "beats"

————————————————————————

```
if MICHIGAN > INDIANA then
    if MICHIGAN > OHIO then
        if INDIANA > OHIO then
            — win prize A
        else
            —— win prize B
    else
        —— win prize C
else
    if MICHIGAN > OHIO then
        if INDIANA > OHIO then
            —— win prize D
        else
            —— win prize E
    else
        —— win prize F
```

Figure 10.3 (continued)

b. *Design Diagram*

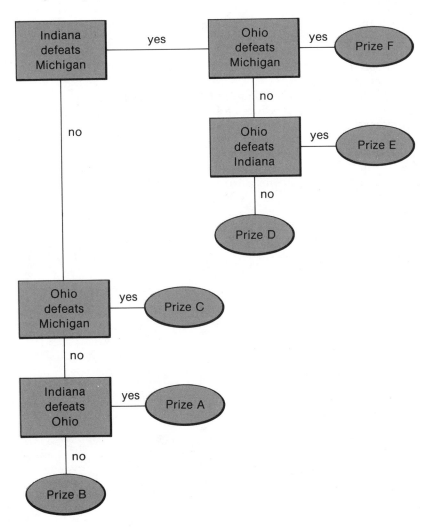

Figure 10.4
Alternative Materials

a. *Another Structured English Format*

There are three games: Ohio versus Michigan, Indiana versus Ohio, and Michigan versus Indiana.
    If Indiana defeats Michigan then
        if Ohio defeats Michigan then you win prize F
        otherwise
            if Ohio defeats Indiana then you win prize E
            otherwise you win prize D
    otherwise
        if Ohio defeats Michigan then you win prize C
        otherwise
            if Indiana defeats Ohio then you win prize A
            otherwise you win prize B

Figure 10.4 (continued)

b. *Another Diagram Format*

Michigan vs. Indiana	Michigan vs. Ohio	Indiana vs. Ohio	
(winner)	(winner)	(winner)	Prize

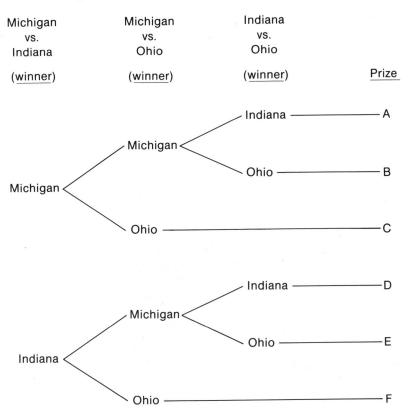

In εgine what reading the program as a whole might be like. Now imagine 50 or 1)0 or 1,000 pages of code in the same spirit and in a systems application.

On the other hand, consider a fragment like:

```
if  (BOARD[SQ1] = PLAYER)
and (BOARD[SQ2] = VACANT) then begin
    if JUMP_AVAILABLE(BOARD, PLAYER) then
        if (LEFT_JUMP_SQ [PLAYER, SQ1] = SQ2)
        or (RIGHT_JUMP_SQ[PLAYER, SQ1] = SQ2) then
            MOVE_STATUS := TEST_JUMP(SQ1, SQ2)
    else
        if (LEFT_SQ [PLAYER, SQ1] = SQ2)
        or (RIGHT_SQ[PLAYER, SQ1] = SQ2) then
            MOVE_STATUS := NONJUMP
e.'d;
```

Now extrapolate to 50 or 1,000 pages of code like this. What would be your reaction? It is certainly in this larger setting that the value of true professional practice will be dramatically demonstrated.

This suggests another approach to measuring the importance of these issues: use programs of some substance. For experimental purposes a reasonable minimum might be 20 pages. This seems long enough to have complicated interactions between procedures, a sizable listing to deal with. Matters of design, consistency, packaging, and global variables start to affect things in earnest. (In a classroom setting, preparing such programs requires more work to produce useful data.)

The kinds of experiments that I think might be useful would be more in the line of user testing. One or more programmers could be given a piece of software and asked to evaluate it. They might be asked to answer questions or, in the extreme, to modify it in some well-defined way. The measures might not be necessarily numeric. We might, for instance, have a study over a period of days or weeks to identify major bottlenecks.

Here is a good place for alternative versions. Practicing programmers almost never see two different programs to solve the same task. When this happens, new insights into the nature of program clarity can be attained. The same problem solved by different programmers or programming teams will generally have widely distinct conventions and protocols, assets and debits.

The setting can be further refined by promoting conscious differences between the programs. One team, for instance, might be responsible for getting as clear and as accurate a design as possible. The other team might be told to finish the program in the shortest possible time. These kinds of situations take on a realism that makes the issues more relevant to professional practice. It is in this setting, I believe, that the issues raised in Volume II of this work are clarified.

The previous discussion centers on two points. First:

- Experimental work can readily be misleading.

Small differences in performance may not seem impressive when, in fact, the issue being tested is indeed of importance. The experiment may measure something that is barely visible in the experiment itself, giving an incorrect or marginal conclusion. Second:

- Experimental work is inherently difficult.

Clear, general results are not easy to achieve. This may explain why empirical work has not had as much impact as we might expect.

11

What Is Successful Software?

In his now classic book, *The Mythical Man-Month,* Frederick Brooks relates his experience in the construction of the OS/360 operating system. In a series of engaging essays, the author describes a number of major lessons learned during the development of this major system. Distributed throughout the world to many thousands (if not a million) users, OS/360 must be considered a major success. But I infer from the book that its development encountered considerable problems—that, perhaps, it was not so successful after all. What, then, is successful software?

More than we wish to admit, some projects are never finished: they languish in the archives of some computer system. These might be called a success if one learned something from the effort.

A completed project could also be considered a success. A project is conceived in one way or another and proceeds toward a conclusion. Along the way, problems intervene. But, in the end, it is completed and finds, perhaps, more than a few users. The developers may call a project a success simply because people use or buy it. But success should mean something more.

A University Project

Consider the following scenario:

> A university is awarded a grant to develop a system that is innovative in the field of computer science. The project examines a new idea that is perceived to be of value not only for the discipline but, in the long run, for industry. The project generates a great deal of enthusiasm as qualified students are hired to begin the implementation. In the background, a thesis and technical reports are begun.
>
> The task is broken into parts and the coding begins. After a year or so, some semblance of a live operation appears. After another six more months, a working version appears. Reports are written, the thesis is completed, and the project is publicized for distribution. A few requests come in and the system is released with some accompanying documentation. After three years, only a handful of people are still using it.

In a project like this, the grounds for judging success may relate to research aspects that are vastly different from the usability or popularity of the system. Some comments.

First, the question of whether one is building a prototype or a piece of software for circulation should be an up-front issue. If things go well, the software might become useful or popular. But this issue should be more a matter of planning than chance.

Second, the software lifecycle needs attention. The management and planning of software is important, even in a university setting. There should exist some kind of clear development sequence, not a situation where events more or less happen. The phases of development, the selection of people to do various tasks, and the isolation of hard benchmarks are paramount considerations.

Finally, the issue of usability should be addressed. If a university project is to be successful as software, the larger environmental concerns must be taken into account. These include well-engineered human interfaces, proper documentation, quality code, and simple installation procedures. These should be just as much a part of a university project as a commercial project. Sometimes we may be teaching students to become sophisticated but not necessarily professional.

There are successes in university endeavors. They can happen, for example, this way:

> A project is conceived and the requirements for the project are extensively analyzed. The scope of the project is scaled down to fit the usually limited

resources of a university, regardless of the generosity of the grant. This limitation is addressed honestly, and overly ambitious features are not attempted.

Next, there is a real production-like flow to the project that is separate from any potential theses that might result. The on-going research issues trail rather than drive the software project. While previous research may be the reason the project is attempted in the first place, the successful completion of the project is the goal.

There can be a great deal of team spirit in a university project—work reading, egoless attitudes, the feeling that there is a definite objective toward a useful product. When the project is finished, there can be a clearly defined period for packaging, promoting, and distributing the work.

When such projects are well conceived and attempt to do something that is a contribution to the research community, requests for the software can flow in for years after the project is completed. The software is not filed in the archives, but has a long and healthy lifetime.

Contract Software

Consider another scenario:

> A project comes up for bids. The project is roughly in the domain of a given organization and there is a strong push to bid on the project. Negotiations proceed, but the bidding organization is on the defensive. Getting the project takes on an importance of its own, even at the sacrifice of resources or design issues considered important. At last, some agreement is reached and the project begins.
>
> It takes a year and half to complete the project. There is some criticism that the project isn't clearly defined, but the project proceeds on its own momentum. There is an initial period when planning, resources, and personnel are placed in order. A working prototype is considered as one of the first goals. The prototype takes longer than planned and becomes the basis for final development.
>
> Certain technical snags get in the way but are resolved. The project takes longer than planned. As the deadline arrives, the project is extended another three months for things to fall into place. The project is finally completed and delivery is made. Most of those involved are relieved to see the project finished.

Let me first say this: *Missing any deadline should be cause for reflection and re-evaluation.* Something is wrong, somewhere.

If someone says a document will be ready on Monday and it isn't finished until Friday, think. Why? Was an unrealistic deadline set? Were there factors beyond control? Why didn't anyone see it? Who might have implicitly counted on Monday and wasted time, paper, or phone calls waiting until Friday? And if someone says a module will be ready next June and it isn't completed and debugged until August, think again. There is waste and disruption from missed deadlines. But, unfortunately, few see it.

A major issue with this scenario is planning. What kinds of projects should an organization attempt? Ideally, there should be a long-range goal for acceptable software contracts. An organization can opt for projects that generate enthusiasm and fit a sensible long-range plan.

Software projects are intrinsically difficult. Understanding the nature of a given application area and getting to the bottom of certain design issues may take years. But, as each project is taken on, a base of resources, equipment, and expertise can be built to handle more projects more successfully. The goal is not piece-work projects but to establish a reputation for producing quality products.

Balancing the economic books today is an understandable objective. But through planning, an organization can focus its attention on quality and direction, optimizing the likelihood that larger profits will follow. Contract software can be a rewarding enterprise in more ways than one.

A Commercial Product

Development of commerical products requires an understanding of timing. Is the market ready for the product? Is it better to introduce a less sophisticated version now or a polished version later? Will a competitor prevail? What is the best price for the product? Difficult considerations indeed.

This is the third scenario.

> The management of the company decides that the time is right to develop product X. There are already plans by competitors to introduce such a product, and any delay may cost them their technical edge in the market place. Resources are made available to plan the effort and to decide the marketing strategy. Engineers are asked to produce preliminary specifications. During the initial planning, a number of new ideas are introduced to give the product more appeal. A date 16 months ahead is set for the initial release. Work begins.
>
> Some new hardware developments may impact the product. Application support groups are also called in to make their recommendations. A number of subsystems are created to go with the product. A common operating system is suggested, and conversion of an existing system for the new software is begun.
>
> Completion of the final software hinges on the skills of several separate groups. Upper-level management is responsible for seeing that integration goes

smoothly. The budget, previously deemed adequate, is now inappropriate and additional resources are added to the project.

As the project continues, it is decided that not all features can be introduced at once. Budgetary constraints are still the controlling factor even with the new resources. An initial release of the system is scheduled. This can be only a minimal system.

A minimal product is released two months after the scheduled date. A year later, the entire system, including documentation, appears on the scene. The project is profitable.

Commercial software development is often the most challenging. First, demands are intense. It is extraordinarily difficult to manage a complex project successfully. Upper-level management, which is often divorced from the technical requirements, may not understand the full scope of the project.

Competing demands lead to a less than optimum strategy. The slippage of schedule, which often calls for pre-releases and pre-pre-releases, leaves the marketplace unsure of what it may expect. The documentation for the project, which should come before coding, barely appears until the end when a litany of inappropriate documentation is often repeated. The scale of the system becomes overwhelming. Individual engineers begin to make separate decisions. Consistency within the project as a whole is lost, and broad interface strategies for users are not realized.

But the test of this scenario is the success of the system. A system that is well conceived should yield a product that is sold over and over again to many satisfied customers. Real profits and real success in a commercial product come from replication. A doubling of the sales can quadruple the profits. Just because the project shows a profit on some accounting basis hardly accounts for what success could have been. The user suffers too. What could have been an artfully crafted product becomes just another mediocre product in the marketplace.

Summary

There is one characteristic of all three scenarios. In each one, the collapse of the software lifecycle is an ominous possibility. Of course, there are worse scenarios. Special note goes to the (not so uncommon) project that simply "disappears." There is little accountability and virtually no lifecycle (not even a collapsing one). The project starts, struggles, then evaporates as though it had never been born.

These scenarios question the meaning of success. This does not mean that a project cannot succeed on various grounds (feasibility, innovation, learning), but, as software, the meaning of success is not always definitive.

Consider the matrix of Figure 11.1. This is a summary of our three hypothetical cases. A second matrix is given in Figure 11.2. This is not only the work of a clear software lifecycle and a true professional team but an indication that the product will indeed be successful.

So, what is successful software? It is a project that has much merit, that generates excitement, whose value is greater than the investment. When the project is completed, no one will have to question whether it is a success or not. It will be obvious to all—the producer and user alike.

Note: An excellent reading for this chapter is the work of [Gould et al., 1986] on the Olympic Message System. From what I understand, this system was a success in a deep sense of the word. User acceptance, actual usage data, requests for similar systems, timeliness—these were all strongly positive.

Figure 11.1
The Three Scenarios

	University Project	*Contract Software*	*Commerical Product*
Source	Grant	Bid	Initiate
Goal	New Idea or Technology	Satisfy Contract	Compete in Marketplace
Specifications	Distributed	Negotiated	Designed
User Documentation	Thesis or Technical Report	User Manual	User Manual
Readability	Inconsequential	Secondary	Variable
Timing	After	After	After
Organization	Research Group	Many individuals	Distributed
Deadline	None	Contracted	In-house
Lifetime Expentancy	Small	Limited	Extended
SUCCESS Factor (1-10)	3 - 5	3 - 5	3 - 5

Figure 11.2
An Ideal Project

	Ideal
Source	N/A
Goal	Project Quality
Specifications	Pre-determined
User Documentation	User Manual
Readability	Primary
Timing	Before
Organization	Integrated Teams
Deadline	Carefully Pre-determined
Lifetime Expectancy	Long
Typical SUCCESS Factor (1-10)	6 — 10

Software Engineering
in
Miniature

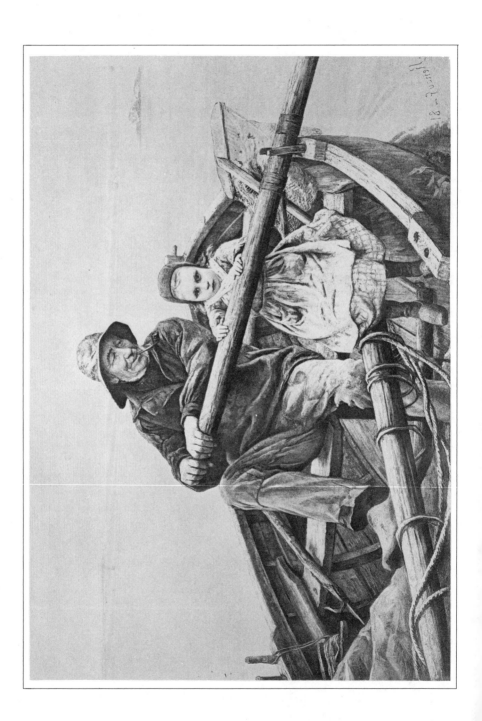

12

A *Small* Demonstration

There is no doubt that software development is an art and, as such, the full scope of its complexity could not be addressed here. This chapter describes the development of a complete, albeit, small example. This example serves pedagogic purposes.

The goal is twofold:

1. To call attention to some of the substantive issues that can occur in practice; and
2. In miniature, at least, to demonstrate parts of a sound development process.

Keep in mind that the example is only suggestive. There are several issues like power and testing that are not covered here. There are also process issues, such as team organization, time pressures, resource limitations, user testing, and management implications, that are beyond the scope of this chapter.

The Example: Text Formatting

The problem is one of conventional text processing. This is the reorganization of a stream of text into a conventional page layout. This involves filling lines so that the lines are more or less balanced on the right, keeping margins, and the printing of page headers. The kind of problem is suggested in Figure 12.1.

In a simple word processing system, for example, the text may contain an embedded control specifying that following lines are to be indented an additional ten spaces from the left margin. The word processing system takes note of this control and, in printing the letter copy, appropriately indents the designated lines. Similarly, in a what-you-see-is-what-you-get editor, the image on the screen is not precisely that which is stored inside the memory of the computer. The computer's copy contains not only the text but additional commands or controls for governing its appearance.

The problem synthesized from these kinds of applications is sketched in Figure 12.2. The input to the program is a file. The file contains text as well as control lines. The control lines govern the layout. The output of the program is a file that is an image of a printed copy, suitably paged and organized. Some arbitrary assumptions are made about its functionality and the environment for which it is written.

Note: The example of this chapter is secondary to the larger goal: software development. Here we consider only a *minimal* text-processing facility. Many valuable features are missing. On the other hand, the example demonstrates how useful an extremely simple but well-crafted user interface can be.

User Interface Issues

Theoretically, software starts with a written document describing the requirements set forth for the potential user. This is the User Requirement Specification (URS, or user specification for short). Why "theoretically"? Because in some cases a URS is never formulated. Software simply grows with informal blessings.

The absence of any written description of the piece of software is often justified on the grounds of expediency or practicality. As new products push technology to a new dimension, writing down even the general requirements may be difficult. In this environment, a prototype may emerge, be refined until eventually the designers are satisfied, then be sent off to market.

Nevertheless, prototype or not, writing the user specification is a necessary task in software development. The effects can be potent: a major obstacle may be resolved, a dead end may be avoided, an expensive feature can be debated, a new philosophy may emerge. The potential gains are many.

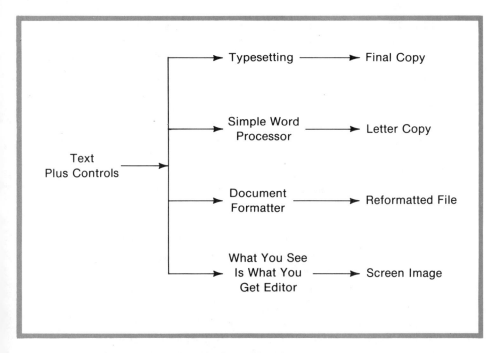

Figure 12.1 Text processing

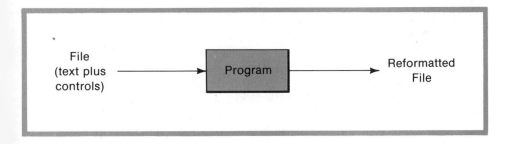

Figure 12.2 The problem

Above its value in sketching the broad outlines of a system, the user specification serves to answer a fundamental question: is the project on or not? The piece of software that was started, consumed resources, yet never made it, may well be the one that never had a clear go-ahead from the start. The user specification forces this issue.

For the text-formatting problem, we assume the existence of a User Requirement Specification. This is given in Figure 12.3. We make the assumption that the document has been generated by management and is taken seriously.

The user requirement of Figure 12.3 is terse and to the point, but hardly complete. Some loose ends are not spelled out. This is typical. The weaknesses of the requirements can, in fact, signal an opportunity because: *The user requirements may well be negotiable.*

User requirements usually stem from sources above the software development team, and there is a tendency to take them literally. The rhetoric may be strong, but the careful software engineer can recognize this hazard. In the text-processing example, the requirements suggest misguided thinking. Let us examine the specification.

The first concern is to question the need for all of the features that are presumed necessary. The command for a new paragraph, for instance, seems unnecessary. The requirements already state that a blank line is assumed to initiate a new paragraph. The difficulty comes when an indented item is printed and a blank line appears after the indented item, but a new paragraph is not called for. This can be handled by assuming that a blank line or a control line terminates the previous paragraph, whether it is an indented item or a normal paragraph.

As for indenting a paragraph, some users prefer no indent (using a blank line to separate paragraphs) or a uniform indent (say five spaces). This option can be easily accommodated. If the user starts a paragraph on the left margin, do not indent. Otherwise (there are one or more leading spaces), use the standard indent. This is a simple solution.

In a minimal facility, it is questionable whether the user really needs to be able to control the standard paragraph indent. A standard paragraph indent of five spaces seems acceptable.

The printing of page headers and page numbers is also problematic. In a limited environment offered by the initial system, there seems little need to give the user control over the position of page headers. A standard, left-justified page header seems sufficient and the page number can be inserted to the left of the header. The single protocol seems sufficient for now, although later versions must address this issue.

Figure 12.3
A User Requirement Specification

Project Title: *A Minimal Basis for Text Processing*

Section 1: *Overview.* The objective of this piece of software is to provide a basis for small, letter-quality printers. The initial requirements call for a minimal facility to handle the organization and printing of a simple report. The initial version will be marketed with the name TEXT.1 and offered at an extremely low price as part of the portable typing terminal.

Section 2: *General Page Layout.* It is assumed that the letter-quality printer will have fixed-pitch spacing at 10 pitch (ten characters per inch). Proportional spacing will not be offered with this version.

All printing is assumed to be done on a standard eight-and-a-half-by-eleven printed page. This means that a line can hold 85 characters and that there are 66 lines on each page. The margins will follow standard typing conventions. This means a left margin of l2 characters, a right margin of 10 characters, a top margin of 8 lines and a bottom margin of 8 lines.

The printing area, thus, becomes 63 characters per line and 50 lines per page. Page numbers are to be inserted on each page except the first. Page numbers are to be printed at the bottom of each page.

Section 3: *Function.* The formatting software will operate on a file of input text. Words in the input stream may have one or more spaces between them. The formatter will see to it that exactly one space is inserted between each word and that lines are filled so that the maximum number of words fits on a single line. In the initial version, there will be no right justification of text.

Blank lines, however, are not to be compressed. A single blank line terminates a paragraph and is to be printed. Sequences of blank lines are also to be printed as they appear.

Section 4: *Style for Layout Controls.* Layout controls are to occupy entire lines. Each control line will begin with a double colon (::). This will ensure that layout commands can be easily isolated. It is expected that the number of layout controls will grow in the future. To relieve typing, each layout command name may be abbreviated by two letters. A single layout control cannot occupy more than a single line.

Section 5: *Design Guidelines.* Enhanced versions of the software are planned, based on the success of initial field testing. User requirements dictate that short control commands are desired by users. The design is also to be modular.

Figure 12.3 (continued)

Section 6: *Layout Controls.* The following layout controls are to appear in the basic release. These are:

::PARA	Starts printing in paragraph style.
::VERBATIM	Starts printing on a literal basis.
::NEW PARA	Calls for the beginning of a new paragraph.
::HEAD "*string*"	Establishes a page header.
::CH	Center the header on the page.
::LH	Left justify the header on the page.
::RH	Right justify the header on the page.
::PAGE	Start a new page.
::DS	Double space the text.
::SS	Single space the text.
::SP *n*	Print *n* blank lines.
::IN *n*	Indent succeeding lines by *n* spaces.
::CENTER *n*	Center the next *n* lines.
::BLOCK ITEM *n*	Print following *n* lines without a page break.
::PARA IN *n*	Establish *n* spaces for paragraph indent.

When a control line that conflicts with a previous control line is given, the most recent control line is to take precedence.

Beyond the overly complex functionality, there are some human engineering issues with the scheme for control lines. The double colon tends to draw attention. In searching for a control line, a user might be tempted to specify a (single) colon as a search string. This conflicts with colons in the text. A more benign character would be the at sign (@).

There also seems to be a concern for the brevity of typing the control lines themselves. This may be misguided. It is more important in this application that the control lines be readable. The control language is a static language rather than an interactive language. The primary design goal should be readability, not brevity of typing. Reading a text file with embedded controls that have been abbreviated poses a burden on the reader every time the control line is read. It seems preferable to spell out each control name in full.

In some interests of brevity, perhaps, the control lines can always be identified with a single name. Thus instead of a command like

@BLOCK ITEM 10

perhaps a syntax like

```
@BLOCK 10
```

or, if compound words can be allowed,

```
@NOSPLIT 10
```

is possible. With this syntax, all control lines can be of the form:

@Control-name optional-argument

This kind of solution may be viewed as a compromise toward readability.

There is some question whether the compromise itself is a reasonable one. For example, should commands like

```
@SET SPACING TO DOUBLE
```

be allowed? This is a major step forward in the readability of the control language, but definitely more complex. In a comprehensive application (for example, typesetting) such a syntax might be justified. We take the simple route here. A resolution to this involves technical matters and design work to find an acceptable syntax in a more powerful setting.

This latter issue has not been resolved in the field of human engineering of computer systems. The language here is a static language (control lines) embedded within another language (the text of the document). This issue needs developmental work in its own right.

As for abbreviations, they are not allowed. These are useful only during input. However, with an eye to easier entry (should a special document editor be allowed for entering the text), all command words and compound command words will be chosen to allow first-letter abbreviation. Thus for example, typing

```
@P
@DS
```

could be used as shorthand entries for

```
@PARAGRAPH
@DOUBLESPACE
```

The longer form would appear in the document.

These concerns lead to a revised list of layout controls, those in Figure 12.4. These are deemed adequate for the initial, minimal application. The revised layout controls must definitely be approved in writing by the appropriate authorities. Here, this means the management commissioning the initial requirements.

Note: The use of the at sign versus the double colon is not an easy issue. While the double colon has some minor technical problems, the at sign on a given typeface can be quite unattractive.

A Developmental User Manual

The following statement is a weary litany: The user manual can wait. Why waste precious time on a sidetrack of dubious value?

Why? Because it works. The user requirement specification has a natural follow-on, the developmental user manual. This is a user manual in the traditional sense, a complete description of the system from the user's point of view. It might, for instance, be used as a guide describing the operation of the system. A careful writing of a user manual requires that many detailed decisions be made that are not apparent in the user specification.

The user manual when done at this initial stage is not an off-hand piece of work. It is *design* at the highest of levels. For instance, in writing a manual, one is forced to specify the way errors are treated, the available options, and, importantly, examples of usage. All of this clarifies the system for its designers. The "whole" is spelled out.

The manual serves another purpose as well. The user requirements are cast in a form that is readable by potential users. The manual can be offered for review, evaluated as a design, and signed off by the project management when it is in an acceptable state. Enough said. The idea speaks for itself. Such a reference manual is given in Figure 12.5.

Figure 12.4
Revised Layout Controls

@SINGLESPACE	Print following text single-spaced (the default)
@DOUBLESPACE	Print following text double-spaced
@HEADER "*string*"	Use *string* as a page header, left justified
@PARAGRAPH	Print following text in paragraph style
@VERBATIM	Print following text as it is given, line by line
@NEWPAGE	Start a new page
@INDENT *n*	Indent following lines by *n* spaces
@CENTER *n*	Center the following *n* lines
@NOSPLIT *n*	Print following *n* lines as a unit, with no page break

Figure 12.5
A Developmental User Manual

TEXT.1
Developmental User Manual

*** DRAFT ***

1. Introduction 2

2. Examples 4

3. Errors 7

4. Invoking TEXT.1 9

Summary of Commands 10

OVERVIEW

TEXT.1 is a program designed to make it easy to enter the text of a document and to print it in a presentable form. The program automatically reformats text so that

1. Lines are filled to the right.
2. Paragraphs have a standard indentation.
3. Page numbers and headers are placed at the top of successive pages of the document.

TEXT.1 is an initial release. Its main application is the production of simple reports, chapters of a book, or any document that is primarily composed of text. It formats the text in a straightforward appearance. It has very few commands. Its primary design goal has been a simple user interface for elementary text preparation.

Figure 12.5 (continued)

— 2 —

1. INTRODUCTION

The writing of a document (for example, a report or a term paper) requires that the text be formatted in a certain style. For example, one must obey certain conventions regarding margins, page numbers, and headers. In addition, the paragraphs should be uniformly indented. Each line should occupy as many words as can fit comfortably within the required margins. TEXT.1 is a simple program designed to make this process convenient and automatic.

The most fundamental operation of TEXT.1 is the spacing of words. For instance, if the input file contains the paragraph

```
Lines can be spaced
arbitrarily.
Extra blanks        can
be left in.    These
will be
taken out when the
paragraph is   formatted.
```

the paragraph will be reformatted as follows:

```
Lines can be spaced arbitrarily. Extra blanks can be
left in. These will be taken out when the paragraph
is formatted.
```

To use this program one must prepare a file containing the document. This text does not have to satisfy the normal conventions required for a neat appearing printed page. The author may wish to keep the document in some reasonably compact and uniform style, but that need not be the case.

In addition to the text, the author may insert control lines. Each control line begins with an at sign (@) and is followed by a single command. The commands govern the final appearance of the text. For instance, the author may insert a command specifying that a sequence of lines is to be indented 10 spaces beyond the normal left margin. The following text will thus be uniformly indented by TEXT.1.

TEXT.1 takes as input a file containing the text of the document and the control lines inserted by the author. As output, TEXT.1 produces a revised copy of the text in another file. This formatted or finished file can be viewed or printed.

The general conventions for the layout of pages are shown in Fig. 1. It is assumed that the document is to be printed on standard 8½-by-11 paper.

Figure 12.5 (continued)

Figure 1.   Page Layout

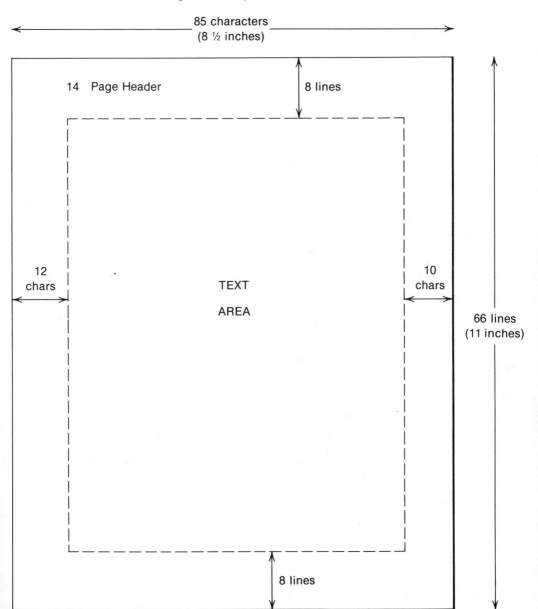

Figure 12.5 (continued)

— 4 —

Margins are kept on the left and right of the text. The top margin contains the page number and any header that the author specifies for the document. The bottom margin is left blank. The text is printed on successive pages beginning on page 1 (which is left unnumbered).

The program assumes the following initial operation:

Spacing: single space
Indentation: none
Page headers: none
Text style: paragraph

This initial setup can be changed, as discussed below.

2.   EXAMPLES

All control lines have the form

@command-name

or

@command-name argument

Control lines always occupy a full line by themselves.

For instance, one can use the NEWPAGE command as follows:

```
The end of a line.
@NEWPAGE
This text will appear on the following page.
```

The NEWPAGE command has no argument and instructs the computer to begin the subsequent text on a new page.

The text of the document will normally appear with single spacing between lines. One may call for double spacing with a command. For example, we may have

```
@DOUBLESPACE
This text will appear in double space.
This means that a blank line will appear
between each line of text.
One can revert to single space with a
new control line.
```

Figure 12.5 (continued)

— 5 —

```
@SINGLESPACE
Back to single space copy, with no blank
lines between lines of text.
```

When this is printed we will see the following:

```
This text will appear in double space. This means

that a blank line will appear between each line of

text. One can revert back to single space with a

new control line.


Back to single space copy, with no blank lines
between lines of text.
```

The printed document can be specified with a header on each page following the first page. For instance, one can say

```
@HEADER "Fundamentals of Running"
```

This command will cause all subsequent pages to be printed with the given header in the upper left-hand corner of the page. Different headers can be inserted at different points in the document by giving subsequent HEADER commands. Note that each header must be enclosed within quotation marks and must fit within a single control line. This means that only single line headers are allowed.

The text of a paragraph is, as one would expect, adjusted so that as many words as possible fit on a single line. For tables, for instance, this is hardly what one would want. For instance, if one entered the lines:

```
ITEM            QUANTITY
Apples          6
Granola         1 lb.
Eggs            1 doz.
```

and did not say anything special, the table would be treated as a paragraph, giving the following:

```
ITEM QUANTITY Apples 6 Granola 1 lb. Eggs 1 doz.
```

To rectify this situation one can use the VERBATIM command. This is done as follows:

Figure 12.5 (continued)

— 6 —

```
@VERBATIM
ITEM           QUANTITY
Apples         6
Granola        1 lb.
Eggs           1 doz.
```

When the VERBATIM command is encountered, all following lines of text are printed exactly as entered. This feature can be used to define not only tables, but equations, inserts, computer programs, and any other text where the spacing is exact. A return to the paragraph style of printing must be explicit. This is done with the PARAGRAPH command.

There are times when the author may wish to indent a fragment of text from the main text. This can be done with an INDENT command, which takes an argument, the number of spaces to be used for the indent. Consider:

```
The last line of a paragraph.

@INDENT 5
Special item 1.

Another special item which
occupies more than one line
and is also indented.

@INDENT 0
This line is not indented.
```

When printed by the system, this fragment will give:

```
The last line of a paragraph.

    Special item 1.

        Another special item which occupies more than
        one line and is also indented.

    This line is not indented.
```

Notice here that even with the indent, the paragraph style is continued.

Titles for tables and headings are often nicely printed in the center of the page. To achieve this effect, one can use the CENTER command. This command also takes an argument, the number of successive lines that are to be centered. Consider:

Figure 12.5 (continued)

— 7 —

```
@CENTER 4
CHAPTER 14

This Is a Title
---------------
```

Here the CENTER command affects the four following lines. When these are printed, the following will appear:

```
        CHAPTER 14

      This Is a Title
      ---------------
```

Suppose we have a diagram or a table that we wish to include within the text. In normal operation TEXT.1 would treat this as any sequence of lines, and should the sequence fall at the end of the page, the diagram or table would be split (i.e. continued on the next page). This can be prevented by using the NOSPLIT command. For example:

```
@VERBATIM
@NOSPLIT 6

           1
         1   1
       1   2   1
     1   3   3   1
   1   4   6   4   1
```

specifies that the triangular numbers are a unit that is not to be split over a page boundary. If the lines happen to fall at the bottom of the page, the item will be printed on the succeeding page.

These examples mention the possible commands that one can insert within a document. The Appendix to this manual gives a more detailed summary of each command.

3.   ERRORS

The available commands are simple and few in number. Nevertheless, even with such a simple control language as offered by TEXT.1, there is room for error. An error will be manifested in one of two ways: (1) TEXT.1 will indicate a problem by printing two asterisks in the left margin of the output; (2) the

Figure 12.5 (continued)

— 8 —

output may not be what was planned or expected. We shall review some of these possibilities here.

   Command errors. In the simplest case, the author may misspell a command word, for example,

   @DUBBLESPACE

When this line is encountered, TEXT.1 will print the control line in the form:

   **   @DUBBLESPACE

and continue processing successive lines as if the command were not given. Thus the output will have a line that was not expected by the author and no double spacing will take effect.
   In a similar vein, if the author inserts the control line

   @INDENT 100   — argument too large

or

   @HEADER (FINAL REPORT"   — ill-formed header

a similar response would result. That is, the erroneous control line would be printed with two asterisks and no action would result.

   Unusual cases. One class of unusual situations can occur when commands have a clear meaning, but that meaning is unlikely to be what the author intends. For example, consider

   @DOUBLESPACE
   @SINGLESPACE

Here the effect of the DOUBLESPACE command is immediately overruled by SINGLESPACE. In this case, the DOUBLESPACE control line will have no net effect. Similarly, consider

   @HEADER "Final Report 1"
   A line of text
   @HEADER "Final Report 2"

where one HEADER is called for and almost immediately followed by a different HEADER. Again, the first HEADER will probably be ignored, unless by some happenstance, the single line of text given between the two header control lines happens to fall on the first line of the page. This sprurious sequence is likely to be erroneous from the author's point of view.

Figure 12.5 (continued)

— 9 —

Next consider,

```
@INDENT 10
@CENTER 1
This Is a Title
```

Here, an indent is called for, immediately followed by a command to center a single line. In this case the title line will be centered, taking the indent into account. Again, this may be an error on the author's part.

An anomoly can also occur with the following sequence.

```
@CENTER 2
This Is a Title
@PARAGRAPH
More text
```

Here, the CENTER command specifies that two lines are to be centered, but one of the lines is itself a control line. In this case, the spurious control line will be flagged with two asterisks to call attention to the problem. The next line will be centered.

These examples are intended to illustrate some of the corners of TEXT.1. Normally, these need not concern the author of a document. The commands are intended to be used during the regular production of a document and such cases are unlikely to arise. They are given here in the event that something spurious from the user's point of view occurs.

4.   INVOKING TEXT.1

In order to make use of the facilities provided by TEXT.1, the user can prepare a file of text using the editor available on the portable typing terminal. The file need not be a complete document as far as the author is concerned, and even fragments from an on-going piece of work can be used.

To have the file processed by TEXT.1, the user simply enters the system command

```
FORMAT file-name
```

As is normal, both uppercase and lowercase letters can be used in system commands. FORMAT can be abbreviated as F.

For example, the following two commands have the same effect:

```
FORMAT SUMMARY
F SUMMARY
```

Figure 12.5 (continued)

— 10 —

The system will use the extension .FMT for the formatted file. For example, in the above case, the formatted file is SUMMARY.FMT.

The formatted file can be viewed on the mini-screen. To print the file, simply enter one of the following:

```
PRINT SUMMARY.FMT
P SUMMARY.FMT
```

Once the printed document is produced, the .FMT file can be deleted from the disk as long as the original text file remains.

Figure 12.5 (continued)

APPENDIX
Summary of Commands

Note: The initial state (the defaults) are: single spacing, paragraph style, no page header, and no indent.

@SINGLESPACE
Specifies that succeeding lines of text are to be printed with single spacing. Single spacing is the default.

@DOUBLESPACE
Specifies that succeeding lines of text are to be printed with double spacing. This includes centered lines and lines governed by NOSPLIT.

@HEADER *"string"*
Specifies that *string* is the text of a header that will appear on subsequent pages. The header will appear at the top left of the page, preceded by the page number. If no header is specified, only the page number is printed.

@PARAGRAPH
Establishes normal paragraph style as the mode of printing. This means filling lines with as many words as possible. A paragraph ends when a blank line or a control line is found. A standard paragraph indent of five spaces is used. This occurs only when the paragraph has at least one leading space; otherwise the first paragraph line is printed flush left.

@VERBATIM
Establishes verbatim style as the mode of printing. This means that lines are printed exactly as given, with no line filling of words.

@NEWPAGE
Forces a page break to occur.

@NOSPLIT *n*
Specifies that the next *n* lines (*n* from 1 through 50) are to be treated as a unit. If fewer than *n* lines remain on the current page, the rest of the page is left blank and the *n* lines are printed at the top of the next page.

@CENTER *n*
Specifies that the next *n* lines (n from 1 through 50) are to be centered.

@INDENT *n*
Specifies that succeeding lines are to be indented *n* spaces from the left margin (*n* from 0 through 50). If *n* is given as 0, no indent is used.

Specification Issues

A user requirement specification, however well intentioned, is usually filled with omissions. The belief that a rough sketch of the software is sufficient to design the initial solution is tempting. The developmental user manual is, however, a preliminary functional specification. It specifies many details of design and casts the project in a clear form.

In the example, there appear to be four broad strategies for the functional specification. These are:

1. Skip it.
2. Define only what is necessary to supplement the user manual.
3. Detail every facet of the system.
4. Write a complete, formal (equation-like) specification.

These broad strategies have the following advantages:

1. The user manual is sufficiently detailed that it may not be worth bothering with any more detailed specification.
2. The user manual contains so much information that it seems wise to supplement it with only the necessary detail to have the system completely defined.
3. Having a single document describing every feature of the system in exact detail is a worthwhile endeavor.
4. Writing a formal description will provide additional help to the programmers in that conventional English prose will be suppressed in favor of a more precise, equation-like description.

Points like these are frequently used to justify whatever path is taken. They are presented here in a positive tone to show just how easy it is to make one's case.

On the other hand, the four broad strategies have the following disadvantages.

1. Going directly to the program itself leaves a number of detailed design decisions in the hands of the programmer. Such decisions will be left to chance, are harder to understand, and much harder to change.
2. Supplementing the user manual leaves a void in the specification. The two together are needed to form a complete mental picture, and this mental picture is not integrated.
3. Writing a single document is a rather overbearing task. It means stating again all of the features described in the user manual in a more precise way. This task may be too tedious for a rational development process.

4. A formal specification adds another dimension, that of trying to find appropriate notations to define the system in a more rigorous way. This can slow down the software development process. It is not clear how much it may, in the end, help the practicing programmer.

This difficulty must be resolved in some reasonable fashion.

For the text-formatting problem, there are a number of questions that are not resolved either in the User Requirements Specification or the User Manual. Some of these are:

- Are words ever truncated?
- What happens if the input file is empty?
- When exactly does a new paragraph begin?
- In what ways do pairs of commands interact; for instance, does a Center command followed immediately by a Verbatim command mean that the lines are to be centered?
- What happens to excessively long input lines?
- What other unusual combinations of commands can occur?
- What happens if a large indent (say 50) is specified under verbatim mode and the line to be printed exceeds the normal line length?
- Are control lines sensitive to blanks?

These are typical questions that often remain unresolved until the final software is written. Yet, they affect the performance of the program and the quality of the result as seen by the user.

In the case of TEXT.1, the specification is not a difficult task. The system is small, a fairly complete manual exists, no hardware interfaces are required, and there are no serious resource constraints. Such facts often require considerable work.

Given the net simplicity of the task, the approach we take is most in line with Item 2, with one exception. Only a broad knowledge of the user manual is assumed. This assumption seems warranted. The user manual is a document that is easily readable. It seems reasonable to assume that someone reading a functional specification, the next level of description of the system, would have access to and be motivated to read the user manual itself.

The reader of the functional specification need not have a line-by-line knowledge of the user manual. This seems too much to ask. Rather, a succinct description of the system will be offered, and its broad context is assumed to be understood.

As for the style of the functional specification, one can take advantage of the smallness of the problem. In particular, *the specification can serve as header comments.* This means avoiding diagrams and symbols that are difficult to include within a program listing. There is little demand here for special notations. This is an advangage: the functional specification can serve double duty. Most programmers do not like writing introductory comments and doing them now will make the programming task easier. This is the choice. The functional specification itself is given in Figure 12.6.

One new issue that writing the functional specification brings up is the method for determining erroneous combinations of commands. There appear to be two broad strategies:

> The extremely tolerant. Try to give a meaning to virtually every combination of commands.

> Forced regularity. Treat dubious command combinations treated as errors and flag them on the output.

Some examples will help.

```
@INDENT 50                          (Case 1)
Long words, like "possibilities,"
present a problem.

@CENTER 2                           (Case 2)
@PARAGRAPH
Now the Title

@NOSPLIT 3                          (Case 3)
@PARAGRAPH
X = 1
Y = 1

@CENTER 10                          (Case 4)
One Line
Another
end-of-file

@INDENT 50                          (Case 5)
@VERBATIM
1 2 3 4 5 6 7 8 9
```

It is instructive to consider these spurious cases in the best possible light. That is, one can try to devise a conceivable circumstance in which the given case is *not* erroneous from the user's point of view. Such interpretations might be:

> *Case 1.* The example, as given, is probably meaningless. However, an indent of 50 may be used to reserve a space for art work, and the text following the control line might be a sequence of brief annotations.

Figure 12.6
A Functional Specification

TEXT.1
Functional Specification

Product Name: TEXT.1

Subject: COMPLETE TECHNICAL SPECIFICATION

Prepared By: Bill Washington
Assisted By: Susan Adams

Date: August 1986

** Overview.   This document describes the behavior of the TEXT.1 document processing system. The system allows the user to prepare a file of text with embedded control lines. Each control line contains a command. The commands specify how the pages of printed text will appear. The output is a new copy of the user's original input text, suitably displayed and formatted. This document assumes a general (not detailed) understanding of the TEXT.1 User Manual.

** Resource Constraints.   There are no particular constraints on the amount of memory required or speed of execution.

** Input.   A file of text containing the text of a document and control lines.

** Output   A file of text that can be viewed or printed directly.

** Sample Input   A sample input to TEXT.1 is as follows:

```
    TEXT.1 is the      basis of a preliminary text
processing system with control lines. The system
assumes that the text contains paragraphs that are
to be displayed in conventional paragraph style.

@INDENT 10
The INDENT command above specifies that the
following text is to be indented 10 spaces from the
left margin. This is what will be printed here.
```

Figure 12.6 (continued)

— 2 —

```
@INDENT 0
@VERBATIM
The VERBATIM control line prints      the lines
exactly as they appear.

         1
        1 1
       1 2 1
      1 3 3 1
     1 4 6 4 1
```

** Sample Output

TEXT.1 is the basis of a preliminary text
processing system with control lines. The system
assumes that the text contains paragraphs which are
to be displayed in conventional paragraph style.

The INDENT command above specifies that
the following text is to be indented 10
spaces from the left margin. This is
what will be printed here.

The VERBATIM control line prints   the lines
exactly as they appear.

```
         1
        1 1
       1 2 1
      1 3 3 1
     1 4 6 4 1
```

** Layout Conventions

```
LINES_PER_PAGE = 66
CHARS_PER_LINE = 85

LEFT_MARGIN   = 12 characters
RIGHT_MARGIN  = 10 characters
```

Figure 12.6 (continued)

— 3 —

```
TOP_MARGIN    = 8 lines
BOTTOM_MARGIN = 8 lines

TEXT_WIDTH    = 63 characters per line
TEXT_LENGTH   = 52 lines per page
PAGE_NUM_LINE = 6 lines from top of page

MAX_INDENT       = 50 characters
MAX_HEADER_WIDTH = 50 characters
MAX_NOSPLIT      = 50 lines
```

** Initial State of System

```
PAGE_HEADER = none
STYLE       = PARAGRAPH
SPACING     = SINGLE
INDENT      = 0
PAGE_NUM    = 1
LINE_NUM    = 1
```

** Commands

SINGLESPACE   The default. Specifies that all subsequent lines are to be printed with single spacing.

DOUBLESPACE   Specifies that succeeding lines are to be printed with double spacing. This applies to lines that are to be centered, lines that are printed verbatim, and lines specified as a block item.

PARAGRAPH   Specifies that a paragraph style is the mode of printing. The first line of each paragraph is either flush left (if no leading spaces are given on input) or is indented five spaces. Once a paragraph is terminated, the next line of text will be taken as the first line of a new paragraph. A paragraph is terminated by a blank line, a control line, or a line with leading spaces.

The words in a paragraph are printed with one space between each word, even if more spaces appear in the input text. The lines of the paragraph (except the last) are word-filled so as to accommodate as many words as possible in the allocated line length. The right margin is ragged edged. An INDENT command specifies an indent for all lines in the paragraph, thus shortening the standard line width.

Figure 12.6 (continued)

— 4 —

VERBATIM   This command changes the style of printing from paragraph style to literal (or verbatim) style. Lines are printed exactly as input, that is medial spaces are kept as on the line of input text.
    Note: If a CENTER command is given in verbatim mode, lines are still centered and verbatim mode takes effect after the centering.

NEWPAGE   Specifies that subsequent text should be printed on a new page beginning on the first line.

HEADER *"string"*   This command specifies a header to be inserted on subsequent pages. Normally, this control line appears at the beginning of the document and affects all pages except the first page, for which no header is printed. If this control line appears after the first page is printed or after a previous control line specifying a header, the newly specified header is used on subsequent pages.

INDENT *n*   Causes a uniform indent of *n* spaces to be used for all succeeding lines. An INDENT command can be used to establish a new indent, or if *n* is zero re-establish the indentation at the left margin. The argument *n* must range from 0 through 50 (barely enough room for even a few words). An indent control affects verbatim lines as well as centered lines. For instance, if an indent of 30 is called for and a CENTER command is later encountered, the lines to be centered will appear midway between the 30th character of a line of text and the right margin.

NOSPLIT *n*   Specifies that the next *n* lines of text are to be treated as a block and not broken over a page boundary. The value of *n* can range from 1 (with no net effect) through 50 (a very large block of unbroken text).

CENTER *n*   Specifies that the next *n* lines are to be centered between the current left margin through the right margin. If leading spaces occur in the lines to be centered, they are countered as characters in the lines to be centered. Trailing spaces, on the other hand, are ignored.

** **Errors.**   The errors flagged fall only in the syntactic category.

  1. Keyword Error. A line begins with an at sign (i.e., presumably a control line) but is not immediately followed by a valid command name.

Figure 12.6 (continued)

— 5 —

2. Header Error. The argument given with a header control is not a properly bracketed string (i.e., the initial or closing quotation mark is missing).

3. Argument Error. The argument for an INDENT or NOSPLIT command is out of range.

   Response: The line is printed as output and flagged with two asterisks in the left margin.

** **Responses to Unusual Situations.**   The philosophy of TEXT.1 is to be as generous as possible when it comes to spurious combinations of input text and commands. If at all possible, some reasonable action is taken. The following situations are unusual, and, thus, require special definition.

1. A control line is within the range of a CENTER or NOSPLIT command.
   Response: Do not count the control line as a line of text, but otherwise act on it.

2. A piece of text extends beyond the right margin.
   Response: Allow the line to extend beyond the right margin. If it happens to extend even beyond the right edge of the paper, print the excess text on the next line.

3. The input file is empty.
   Response: One page is output with an error diagnostic.

4. The text to be centered has leading spaces.
   Response: Use the leading spaces as part of the text.

5. NOSPLIT is applied to paragraphed text.
   Response: Treat as normal. This may mean that the argument n given with NOSPLIT may not be exact, since line-filling in paragraph mode can change the number of output lines.

Case 2. These control lines might appear at the beginning of a document and specify that the first two lines of text will be title lines and that paragraph style is to be used in the document.

Case 3. The absence of a blank line after each equation means that the equations will be pushed onto a single line. This is most likely an error. But one might imagine a special paragraph that should not be split.

Case 4. This case might arise if the user is midway through a document, gets interrupted after two centered lines are given, and terminates entry to get an intermediate copy.

Case 5. Here, again, the given example is unreasonable. But, conceivably, for emphasis, the author of a document may wish the line to extend beyond the right margin.

While these cases are far fetched, the question is whether to give a user the freedom to exercise these unusual combinations.

It can be argued that the cases are unreasonable and, in fact, errors on the user's part. Is it better to force a certain regularity on the use of the control language so that spurious combinations are flagged?

In programming, it is important to use constructs in a regular manner. A good programmer would stay away from strange constructs and consider them as poor practice. Hence, there is a predisposition to consider the preceding cases as downright errors—to be flagged as such.

On the other hand, some of these spurious cases will be obvious to the author. For example, the output when a word exceeds the right margin is visible. There seems little reason to call any more attention to such cases. Second, there will probably be a class of users who find the spurious cases quite normal. They will object to having these cases flagged as errors, with some annoying (to them) mark on the printed copy. Even though the command facilities are limited, there seems little reason to stifle the adventuresome author who wishes to make use of these combinations or the careless author who does not pay too much attention to the sequence in which control lines are given.

So, with some hesitation, none of the preceding cases will be considered as errors. This leaves only one class of error, and that is a control line that is not syntactically well formed. For example,

```
@DUBBLESPACE
```

or

```
@HEADER "Final Report
```

These syntactic errors are the only ones that will be flagged on the user's output, for the system itself cannot really interpret them.

Note: This decision, in effect, changes what was written in the developmental user manual. This kind of change needs approval from management and should be recorded in an updated version. Here, again, one general point: the description of the system, when done beforehand, is *not* neutral to design. It not only clarifies the design but points out cases that need further analysis.

Program Design

The objective so far has been to define the problem at hand in complete and unambiguous detail. The user requirements, the user manual, and the functional specification have served several purposes. They should, accordingly, be signed for approval. We are now ready to consider how we would implement such a program in broad terms.

At this stage, we harken the programmer to beware of this—Trap: *I'll just get the I/O routines going.* Barring the need for a prototype and possible user testing (matters we do not address here), it is the time to consider the overall program design. In our case, this means: What is the overall strategy for processing input lines? There are many solutions.

The first thought that comes to mind is to examine the input on a character-by-character basis, taking action after each character. This solution is obviously faulty. There is a deeper structure to an input file than a string of characters. The file is a sequence of lines. There are two distinct kinds of lines: text and control. At the very least, the general strategy is to work on a line-by-line basis.

But this itself does not really resolve the problem. One could take the solution,

```
READ (line)
PROCESS (line)
PRINT (line)
```

This is a scenario familiar to all programmers. It, too, has problems. First, an input line does not have a one-to-one correspondence with an output line. Paragraphs must be line-filled with words, and several input lines may correspond to one output line. Moreover, control lines affect subsequent text lines. The CENTER control line has a different impact on subsequent lines than the PARAGRAPH control line has

Figures 12.7, 12.8, and 12.9 outline three broad strategies for text analysis.

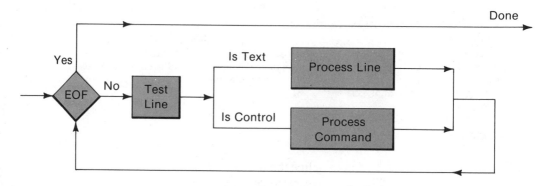

Figure 12.7 Line based

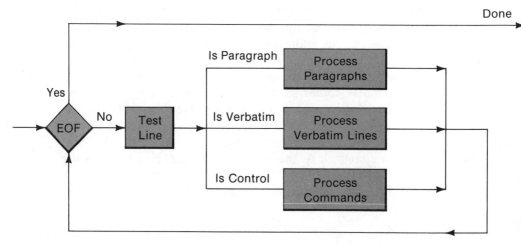

Figure 12.8 Mode based

Design A—Line by line. In this design, the lines for input are examined one by one. Based on the type of line (text versus control), the line is processed by a subroutine. Flow of control returns to the top level of the program after each line is processed.

Design B—Mode based. In this design, the current line dictates a call to one of three subroutines. One will process commands until a text line is reached. A second will process verbatim lines until a control line is

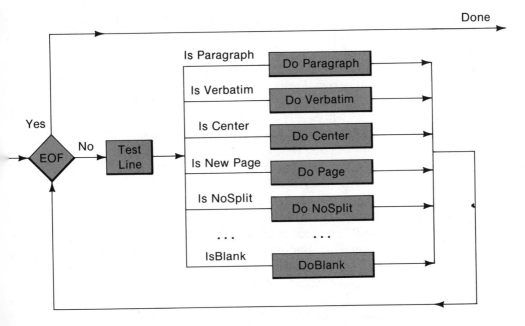

Figure 12.9 Control-line based

reached. The third will process paragraph lines until a control line is reached. The design continues in one mode (for example, processing paragraph lines) until something causes the mode to change.

Design C—Control-line based. In this design, the current line is tested. A determination is made to see if it is the start of a new paragraph, a new verbatim block, a group of lines to be centered, a page break, and so forth. Based on this choice, one of about ten subroutines will be called to handle the case in question. Control will then revert to the top level.

Obviously, each design assumes certain global information needed to complete its definition (for example, variables that give the status of each tested line). A few remarks on each of the designs is in order.

Design A is the least comprehensive of the three in that it entails only a simple decomposition of the problem. The line orientation seems in keeping with the observation that control lines may appear at any point in the input file. However, it poses some questions. For one, some type of buffer is needed to store lines of text as they are being built. The detection of a control line that will terminate a paragraph requires that the buffered input line be output separately. For another, it means that a good deal of global state information must be kept. This information must be passed down to the relevant procedures for handling line centering or block items. This design, in particular, needs amplification.

The mode-based design, Design B, has something to be said for it. It is likely that the input file will match its style of working with groups of lines. For instance, one frequent case is a long sequence of paragraphs. These will be handled all at once, in a separate subroutine. But the difficulty with this design is that the processing of control lines is not quite as simple as it appears. For example, in centering or in handling block items, the input lines to be processed may be interrupted by embedded control lines.

Design C, the control-line based, is appealing. On closer inspection, however, it is not clear that it works. Implicit in this design is that each of the procedures will handle one case completely (for instance, all verbatim lines or all lines to be centered). But a subroutine to do centering, for example, may encounter a new control line, say, a new page command. Similarly, verbatim lines may be temporarily centered or indented and thus require a return to the outer level. This seems inconsistent with the intent of the design.

A hard case for any of the designs is the following:

```
@CENTER 3
first line of title
@NOSPLIT 4
second line
third line
fourth line
fifth line
```

The interpretation given to this strange sequence is that three lines are to be centered, but, after centering the first line, the remaining two lines to be centered and the subsequent two lines must not appear split across a page boundary. This example is instructive in that it shows the depth to which any design must be examined.

Design B, thus, seems the most attractive, but, on closer inspection, there are some uncomfortable points. First, there seems little reason to process commands as a group when control always goes back to the main algorithm. As is, control will switch between (a) commands and (b) one of the two other choices.

Second, the method of centering is odd. Centered lines come in groups, just as do verbatim and paragraph lines. The groups may be smaller, but, nevertheless, the centering command affects subsequent lines in a way commands like PAGE and NOSPLIT do not. Perhaps centering should be handled on the same basis as verbatim and paragraph lines.

But wait. This implies that the CENTER command should *not* have an argument! Rather, it should set a mode just as do PARAGRAPH and VERBATIM. This is a change to the *specification*. The idea seems to be a good one for both the user and implementor. It must be approved.

So, a cleaner formulation of the design is given in Figure 12.10. This design now has a more pleasant symmetry. Control lines can be processed one by one, and, then periodically, a shift will occur in which a group of lines will be processed. A rough sketch of the algorithm corresponding to Figure 12.10 is as follows:

```
INDENTATION := 0;
MODE        := PARAGRAPH_STYLE;

while MORE_DATA(INFILE) do begin

    if NEXT_CHAR(INFILE) = CONTROL_CHAR then
        DO_COMMAND_LINE ({updating} MODE, INDENTATION,
                                    INFILE, OUTFILE, PAGE)

    else if MODE = PARAGRAPH_STYLE then
        FORMAT_PARAGRAPHS ({using}   INDENTATION,
                           {updating} INFILE, OUTFILE, PAGE)

    else if MODE = VERBATIM_STYLE then
        COPY_VERBATIM ({using}   INDENTATION,
                       {updating} INFILE, OUTFILE, PAGE)

    else {MODE = CENTERED}
        CENTER_LINES ({using}   INDENTATION,
                      {updating} INFILE, OUTFILE, PAGE)
end;
```

This version of the algorithm indicates that some additional variables are needed to specify the actions completely.

Program Decomposition

It is instructive now to consider how one would organize the program into independent packages that can be written by different programmers. This is part of the overall design—Trap: *Put the widely used constants and types in a package.* A programmer may jump to a hasty conclusion by using the following packages: I/O routines, global constants and types, utility routines, and control routines. The difficulty with this decomposition is that

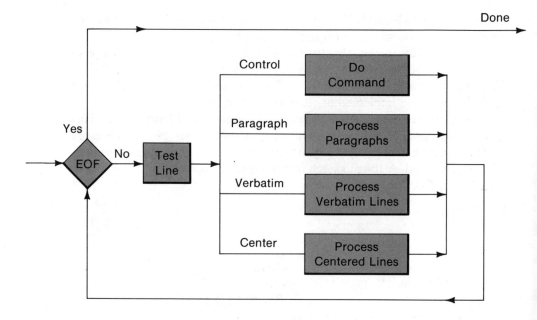

Figure 12.10 The overall design

it is not based on the *problem*. Rather, it is more syntactic, more implementation based. Putting all of the types together does not isolate the information for a given topic. The same could be said for utility routines. Just because the routines are used frequently or are at the lowest calling level hardly justifies their status as a module.

One candidate for a package is all the information needed about page layout. This is the set of constants, types, and procedures that encapsulate what the user needs to know about the printing of pages. From the user's point of view, there are several important page layout constants. These include:

```
LINES_PER_PAGE    (66 lines)
TEXT_WIDTH        (63 characters)
PARA_INDENT       (5 characters)
```

Moreover, the user needs to interface with several procedures. These include:

```
START_DOCUMENT    -- Set up first page
FINISH_DOCUMENT   -- Finish off last page
```

```
NEXT_LINE            -- Start a new line
NEXT_PAGE            -- Start a new page
PRINT_ERROR_LINE     -- Print an erroneous control line
PRINT_TEXT_LINE      -- Print a line of text
```

The objective is to characterize some definite knowledge that can be isolated on its own and provide a simple interface to program units that need this knowledge.

In the above case, that of page layout, the decisions are not completely clear cut.

- Is the interface as simple as possible?
- Does it partition the software with a clear boundary?
- Does it take into account the needs of various users?

These issues are never easy.

After much consideration, the following general decomposition was taken.

A main program, which handles the basic command routines and the formatting of text.

A package named INPUT_INFO, which provides the interface for getting lines of text from the input file.

A package named CONTROL_LINES, which handles the parsing of control lines.

A package named PAGE_LAYOUT, which controls the printing of pages in the desired format.

The packages may be viewed as support items for the main program. A sketch of the proposed decomposition is given in Figure 12.11. The complete program is given in the Appendix.

Note: In Volume II of this work, the program is again presented—this time with annotations. The annotations discuss programming practice issues in the context of the example program.

Lessons

A user requirement was stated, negotiated, and revised. Then, a developmental user manual was written. This, presumably, was the full specification at a user-level of detail.

Next a functional specification was written. It revealed a change (in the error strategy) to the User Manual. Still later, the design process resulted in

Figure 12.11
Overall Decomposition

```
program TEXT1 (INFILE, OUTFILE);
inherit INPUT_INFO, PAGE_LAYOUT, CONTROL_LINES;
   -- declarations for main program
begin
   -- statements of main program
end.

{ ----------------------------------------------------------- }

package INPUT_INFO;
   const
      MAX_LINE_WIDTH = 120;
      CONTROL_CHAR   = '@';

   . . .

   procedure GET_LINE (var INFILE: TEXT; var LINE: LINE_INFO);
   procedure GET_WORD (var INFILE: TEXT; var WORD: LINE_INFO);
end;

{ ----------------------------------------------------------- }

package CONTROL_LINES;
inherit INPUT_INFO;
   const
      MAX_INDENT       = 50;
      MAX_HEADER_WIDTH = 50;

   . . .

   procedure PARSE_CONTROL_LINE ({using} LINE: LINE_INFO;
                                 {giving} var CMD: COMMAND_INFO);
end;

{ ----------------------------------------------------------- }

package PAGE_LAYOUT;
inherit INPUT_INFO;
   const
      { -- Vertical }
      LINES_PER_PAGE = 66;
      TOP_MARGIN     = 8;

   . . .

   procedure SET_NO_SPLIT (NUM_LINES: INTEGER;
                           var OUTFILE: TEXT; var PAGE: PAGE_INFO);
   procedure SET_SPACING  (OPTION: SINGLE_OR_DOUBLE);
                           var PAGE: PAGE_INFO);
end;

{ ----------------------------------------------------------- }
```

another change (deleting the argument for a CENTER command). Does this undermine the process taken?

Not at all. On the contrary, the process ensures stability. What would things have been like if (as is frequent) we had not had this mini-lifecycle? The changes are few in number and visible to all. Good engineering has elements of art, science, and compromise.

Some common problems that the extended example illustrates can be summarized as follows:

1. This is a failure to question, simplify, or improve the user requirements.
2. The developmental user manual is deemed unnecessary.
3. The functional specification is chancy.
4. Design is hurried.
5. Decomposition is often not based on problem-oriented terms.
6. Coding is rushed and sporadic in quality.

Put in the positive, it comes out like this:

1. Negotiate the requirements.
2. Write the user manual first.
3. Write a complete technical specification.
4. Consider alternative designs.
5. Decompose the software by looking at the problem.
6. Write beautiful and meaningful code.

These are major points. They are keys to our profession.

Appendix

The Example Program

```
{ -- ** Product Name:  TEXT.1

  -- ** Programmed by:  Bill Washington
  -- ** Assisted by:    Susan Adams
  -- ** Date: November 1986

  -- ** Overview: The TEXT.1 document processing system allows the
  -- user to prepare a file of text with embedded control lines.
  -- Each control line contains a command. The commands specify how
  -- the pages of printed text will appear. The output is a new copy
  -- of the user's original input text, suitably displayed and
  -- formatted. This document assumes a general (not detailed)
  -- understanding of the TEXT.1 User Manual.

  -- ** Resource Constraints: There are no particular constraints on
  -- this program as regards the amount of memory required for storage
  -- or the speed at which the program must execute.
```

```
--  ** Input: A file of text, which contains the text of a
--  document and control lines.

--  ** Output: A file of text, which can be viewed or printed
--  directly.



--  ** Layout Conventions:

--  * Vertical
--  LINES_PER_PAGE = 66
--  TOP_MARGIN      =  8 lines
--  BOTTOM_MARGIN   =  8 lines
--  TEXT_LENGTH     = 50 lines per page
--  MAX_NOSPLIT     = 50 lines
--  PAGE_NUM_LINE   =  6 lines from top of page

--  * Horizontal
--  CHARS_PER_LINE   = 85
--  LEFT_MARGIN      = 12 characters
--  RIGHT_MARGIN     = 10 characters
--  TEXT_WIDTH       = 63 characters per line
--  MAX_INDENT       = 50 characters
--  MAX_HEADER_WIDTH = 50 characters




--  ** Sample Input:

--          TEXT.1 is the       basis of a preliminary text
--      processing system with control lines. The system
--      assumes that the text contains paragraphs that are
--      to be displayed in conventional paragraph
--      style.

--      @INDENT 10
--      The INDENT control line above specifies that the
--      following text is to be indented 10 spaces from the
--      left margin. This is what will be printed here.
```

```
--      @INDENT 0
--      @VERBATIM
--      The VERBATIM control line prints      the lines
--      exactly as they appear.
--              1
--             1 1
--            1 2 1
--           1 3 3 1
--          1 4 6 4 1


-- ** Sample Output:

--          TEXT.1 is the basis of a preliminary text
--      processing system with control lines. The system
--      assumes that the text contains paragraphs that are
--      to be displayed in conventional paragraph style.

--                The INDENT control line above specifies
--                that the following text is to be indented
--                10 spaces from the left margin. This is
--                what will be printed here.

--      The VERBATIM control line prints      the lines
--      exactly as they appear.
--              1
--             1 1
--            1 2 1
--           1 3 3 1
--          1 4 6 4 1


-- ** Initial State of System:

-- PAGE_HEADER = none
-- MODE        = PARAGRAPH_STYLE
-- SPACING     = SINGLE
-- INDENTATION = 0
-- PAGE_NUM    = 1
-- LINE_NUM    = 1
```

```
-- ** Control Line Commands:

-- SINGLESPACE    The default. Specifies that all subsequent lines
-- are to be printed with single spacing.

-- DOUBLESPACE    Specifies that succeeding lines are to be printed
-- with double spacing. This applies to lines that are to be
-- centered, printed verbatim, and block items.

-- PARAGRAPH    Specifies that paragraph style is the mode of
-- printing. The first line of each paragraph is either flush left
-- (if no leading spaces are given on input) or is indented 5 spaces.
-- A paragraph is terminated by a blank line, a control line, or a
-- line with leading spaces. Once a paragraph is terminated, the next
-- line of text will be taken as the first line of a new paragraph.
--      The lines of the paragraph (except the last) are word-filled
-- so as to accommodate as many words as possible. The right margin
-- is ragged edged. An INDENT command specifies an indent for all
-- lines in the paragraph, thus shortening the standard line width.

-- VERBATIM    This command changes the style of printing to literal
-- (or verbatim) style. Lines are printed exactly as input. An INDENT
-- command causes a verbatim line to be shifted to the right.

-- CENTER    Specifies that the following lines are to be centered
-- between the current left margin and the right margin. If leading
-- spaces occur in the lines to be centered, they are counted as
-- characters in the lines to be centered. Trailing spaces, on the
-- other hand, are ignored.

-- NEWPAGE    Specifies that subsequent text should be printed on a
-- new page, beginning on the first line.

-- HEADER "string"    This command specifies a header to be inserted
-- on subsequent pages. Normally this control line will appear at the
-- beginning of the document and affects all pages except the first
-- page, for which no header is printed. If this control line appears
-- after the first page is printed or after a previous control line
-- specifying a header, the newly specified header is used on
-- subsequent pages.
```

```
-- INDENT n    Causes a uniform indent of n spaces to be used for
-- all succeeding lines. If n is zero, re-establishes the indentation
-- at the left margin. The argument n must range from 0 through 50
-- (barely enough room for even a single word). An indent command
-- affects verbatim lines as well as centered lines. For instance, if
-- an indent of 30 is called for and a CENTER command is later
-- encountered, the centered lines will appear midway between the 30th
-- character of a line of text and the right margin.

-- NOSPLIT n    Specifies that the succeeding n lines of text are
-- to be treated as a block and not broken over a page boundary. The
-- value of n can range from 1 (with no net effect) through 52 (a
-- very large block of unbroken text).



-- ** Errors:

--      Only syntactic errors are detected. There are:

--      1. Keyword Error. A line from the input file begins with an
--         at sign (i.e., presumably a control line) but is not
--         followed by one the command names.
--      2. Header Error. The argument given with a header command is
--         not a properly bracketed string (i.e., the initial or closing
--         double quotation mark is missing).
--      3. Argument Error. The argument for an INDENT or NOSPLIT
--         command is out of range.

--      Response: The line is printed as output and flagged with two
--      asterisks in the left margin.


-- ** Responses to Unusual Situations:

--      The philosophy of TEXT.1 is to be as generous as possible
-- when it comes to spurious combinations of input text and commands.
-- If at all possible, some reasonable action is taken. The
-- following situations are unusual and thus require special
-- definition.
```

```
--      1. A control line appears within the range of a NOSPLIT
--         command.
--      Response: Process it as a control line, but do not count it
--      as a line of text for NOSPLIT.

--      2. A piece of text extends beyond the right margin.
--      Response: Allow the line to extend beyond the right margin.
--      If it happens to extend even beyond the right edge of the
--      paper, excess text is printed on the next line.

--      3. The input file is empty.
--      Response: One page is output, with an error diagnostic
--      printed on it.

--      4. Text to be centered has leading spaces.
--      Response: Use the leading spaces as part of the text. The
--      assumption here is the user wants them (e.g., wants to
--      move a header slightly off center). The user can always
--      delete the spaces.

--      5. NOSPLIT is applied to paragraphed text.
--      Response: Treat as normal. This may mean that the argument
--      n given with NOSPLIT may not be exact, since line-filling
--      in paragraph mode can change the number of output lines.  }


{  ------------------------------------------------------  }
```

```
program TEXT_1 (INFILE, OUTFILE);

inherit INPUT_INFO, PAGE_LAYOUT, CONTROL_LINES;

    const
       BLANK = ' ';

    type
       TEXT_MODE = (PARAGRAPH_STYLE, VERBATIM_STYLE, CENTERED);

    var
       INFILE, OUTFILE: TEXT;
       MODE:            TEXT_MODE;
       INDENTATION:     INTEGER;
       PAGE:            PAGE_INFO;



procedure ADD_TEXT ({using} LINE: LINE_INFO;
                    {to}     var BUFFER: TEXT_INFO);
{ -- This procedure appends the text in LINE to the text buffer. }
    var
       I: INTEGER;

begin
    for I := 1 to LINE.WIDTH do
       BUFFER.IMAGE[BUFFER.WIDTH + I] := LINE.IMAGE[I];

    BUFFER.WIDTH := BUFFER.WIDTH + LINE.WIDTH
end;




procedure ADD_SPACES ({using}    NUM_SPACES:   INTEGER;
                      {updating} var BUFFER: TEXT_INFO);
{ -- This procedure adds spaces to the text buffer. }
    var
       I: INTEGER;

begin
    for I := 1 to NUM_SPACES do
       BUFFER.IMAGE[BUFFER.WIDTH + I] := BLANK;

    BUFFER.WIDTH := BUFFER.WIDTH + NUM_SPACES
end;
```

```
procedure CENTER_LINES ({using}     INDENTATION: INTEGER;
                        {updating} var INFILE:  TEXT;
                                   var OUTFILE: TEXT;
                                   var PAGE:    PAGE_INFO);

{ -- This procedure takes lines from the input file and centers
  -- them on the output file. Leading spaces on input lines are
  -- counted as text for centering. The indentation is used as
  -- the left margin for centering. }

   var
      LINE:       LINE_INFO;
      BUFFER:     TEXT_INFO;
      PADDING:    INTEGER;
      PRINT_WIDTH: INTEGER;

begin
   BUFFER.WIDTH := 0;
   while MORE_DATA(INFILE)
   and (NEXT_CHAR(INFILE) <> CONTROL_CHAR) do begin
      GET_LINE (INFILE, LINE);
      ADD_SPACES (INDENTATION, BUFFER);

      PRINT_WIDTH := TEXT_WIDTH - INDENTATION;
      if LINE.WIDTH < PRINT_WIDTH then
         begin
            PADDING := (PRINT_WIDTH - LINE.WIDTH) div 2;
            ADD_SPACES (PADDING, BUFFER)
         end;

      ADD_TEXT (LINE, BUFFER);
      PRINT_TEXT_LINE (BUFFER, OUTFILE, PAGE)
   end
end;
```

```
procedure COPY_VERBATIM ({using}      INDENTATION: INTEGER;
                         {updating} var INFILE:  TEXT;
                                    var OUTFILE: TEXT;
                                    var PAGE:    PAGE_INFO);

{ -- This procedure copies lines from the input file to the output file,
  -- adding the current indentation to each output line. }

    var
        LINE:   LINE_INFO;
        BUFFER: TEXT_INFO;

begin
    BUFFER.WIDTH := 0;
    while MORE_DATA(INFILE)
    and (NEXT_CHAR(INFILE) <> CONTROL_CHAR) do begin
        GET_LINE (INFILE, LINE);
        ADD_SPACES (INDENTATION, BUFFER);
        ADD_TEXT (LINE, BUFFER);
        PRINT_TEXT_LINE (BUFFER, OUTFILE, PAGE)
    end
end;
```

```
procedure PROCESS_WORD ({using} INDENTATION: INTEGER;
                                 WORD: LINE_INFO;
                     {updating} var BUFFER:  TEXT_INFO;
                                var OUTFILE: TEXT;
                                var PAGE:    PAGE_INFO);

{ -- This procedure handles a single word. }

begin
    if (WORD.WIDTH + BUFFER.WIDTH) <= TEXT_WIDTH then
        begin
            ADD_TEXT (WORD, BUFFER);
            ADD_SPACES (1, BUFFER)
        end
    else if (WORD.WIDTH + INDENTATION) <= TEXT_WIDTH then
        begin
            PRINT_TEXT_LINE (BUFFER, OUTFILE, PAGE);
            ADD_SPACES (INDENTATION, BUFFER);
            ADD_TEXT (WORD, BUFFER);
            ADD_SPACES (1, BUFFER)
        end
    else
        begin
            if BUFFER.WIDTH > INDENTATION then
                begin
                    PRINT_TEXT_LINE (BUFFER, OUTFILE, PAGE);
                    ADD_SPACES (INDENTATION, BUFFER)
                end;
            ADD_TEXT (WORD, BUFFER);
            PRINT_TEXT_LINE (BUFFER, OUTFILE, PAGE);
            ADD_SPACES (INDENTATION, BUFFER)
        end
end;
```

```
procedure FORMAT_PARAGRAPHS ({using} INDENTATION: INTEGER;
                              {updating} var INFILE:  TEXT;
                                         var OUTFILE: TEXT;
                                         var PAGE:    PAGE_INFO);

{ -- This procedure reformats text into whole paragraphs. It keeps
  -- processing input lines until a control line is reached. }

   var
      LINE:   LINE_INFO;
      WORD:   LINE_INFO;
      BUFFER: TEXT_INFO;

begin
   BUFFER.WIDTH := 0;
   ADD_SPACES (INDENTATION, BUFFER);
   while MORE_DATA(INFILE)
   and (NEXT_CHAR(INFILE) <> CONTROL_CHAR) do begin
      if EOLN(INFILE) then { -- empty input line }
         begin
            if BUFFER.WIDTH > INDENTATION then
               PRINT_TEXT_LINE (BUFFER, OUTFILE, PAGE);
            READLN (INFILE);
            NEXT_LINE (OUTFILE, PAGE);
            ADD_SPACES (INDENTATION, BUFFER)
         end
      else
         begin
            if NEXT_CHAR(INFILE) = BLANK then { -- new paragraph }
               begin
                  if BUFFER.WIDTH > INDENTATION then
                     PRINT_TEXT_LINE (BUFFER, OUTFILE, PAGE);
                  ADD_SPACES (INDENTATION + PARA_INDENT, BUFFER)
               end;
            GET_WORD (INFILE, WORD);
            while WORD.WIDTH <> 0 do begin
               PROCESS_WORD (INDENTATION, WORD, BUFFER, OUTFILE, PAGE);
               GET_WORD (INFILE, WORD)
            end;
            READLN(INFILE)
         end
   end;

   if BUFFER.WIDTH > INDENTATION then
      PRINT_TEXT_LINE (BUFFER, OUTFILE, PAGE)
end;
```

```
procedure DO_COMMAND_LINE ({updating} var MODE:         TEXT_MODE;
                                       var INDENTATION: INTEGER;
                                       var INFILE:      TEXT;
                                       var OUTFILE:     TEXT;
                                       var PAGE:        PAGE_INFO);

{ -- This procedure extracts a control line from the input file and acts
  -- upon it. }

   var
      LINE: LINE_INFO;
      CMD:  COMMAND_INFO;

begin
   GET_LINE (INFILE, LINE);
   PARSE_CONTROL_LINE (LINE, CMD);

   case CMD.NAME of
      SINGLESPACE: SET_SPACING (SINGLE, PAGE);

      DOUBLESPACE: SET_SPACING (DOUBLE, PAGE);

      HEADER:      SET_HEADER (CMD.STRING_ARG, CMD.STRING_LEN, PAGE);

      NEWPAGE:     NEXT_PAGE (OUTFILE, PAGE);

      PARAGRAPH:   MODE := PARAGRAPH_STYLE;

      VERBATIM:    MODE := VERBATIM_STYLE;

      CENTER:      MODE := CENTERED;

      INDENT:      INDENTATION := CMD.NUMERIC_ARG;

      NOSPLIT:     SET_NOSPLIT (CMD.NUMERIC_ARG, OUTFILE, PAGE);

      ERROR:       PRINT_ERROR_LINE (LINE, OUTFILE, PAGE)
   end
end;
```

```
begin { -- Main program }
   RESET (INFILE);
   REWRITE (OUTFILE);

   INDENTATION := 0;
   MODE := PARAGRAPH_STYLE;
   START_DOCUMENT (OUTFILE, PAGE);

   while MORE_DATA(INFILE) do begin

      if NEXT_CHAR(INFILE) = CONTROL_CHAR then
         DO_COMMAND_LINE ({updating} MODE,  INDENTATION,
                                     INFILE, OUTFILE, PAGE)

      else if MODE = PARAGRAPH_STYLE then
         FORMAT_PARAGRAPHS ({using}    INDENTATION,
                            {updating} INFILE, OUTFILE, PAGE)

      else if MODE = VERBATIM_STYLE then
         COPY_VERBATIM ({using}    INDENTATION,
                        {updating} INFILE, OUTFILE, PAGE)

      else { -- MODE = CENTERED }
         CENTER_LINES ({using}    INDENTATION,
                       {updating} INFILE, OUTFILE, PAGE)
   end;

   FINISH_DOCUMENT (OUTFILE, PAGE)
end.


{ ------------------------------------------------------ }
```

```
package INPUT_INFO;

   const
     MAX_LINE_WIDTH = 120;
     CONTROL_CHAR   = '@';

   type
     LINE_IMAGE = packed array [1..MAX_LINE_WIDTH] of CHAR;
     LINE_INFO =
        record
          WIDTH: 0..MAX_LINE_WIDTH;
          IMAGE: LINE_IMAGE
        end;

   function MORE_DATA (var INFILE: TEXT): {returns} BOOLEAN;
   function NEXT_CHAR (var INFILE: TEXT): {returns} CHAR;

   procedure GET_LINE (var INFILE: TEXT; var LINE: LINE_INFO);
   procedure GET_WORD (var INFILE: TEXT; var WORD: LINE_INFO);
end;



{ ------------------------------------------------------- }
```

```
package body INPUT_INFO;


function MORE_DATA(var INFILE: TEXT):  {returns} BOOLEAN;
begin
  if EOF(INFILE) then
      MORE_DATA := FALSE
    else
      MORE_DATA := TRUE
end;



function NEXT_CHAR(var INFILE: TEXT): {returns} CHAR;

{ -- A slight trick is needed here to simulate an end of file or an
  -- end of line. }

   const
      NULL_CHAR = CHR(0);

begin
   if EOF(INFILE) then
      NEXT_CHAR := NULL_CHAR
    else if EOLN(INFILE) then
      NEXT_CHAR := NULL_CHAR
    else
      NEXT_CHAR := INFILE↑
end;
```

```
procedure GET_LINE ({from} var INFILE: TEXT;
                    {into} var LINE:   LINE_INFO);

{ -- This procedure obtains the next line of the input file and
  -- deletes any trailing blanks. }

    var
        I: INTEGER;
        TRAILING_BLANKS: BOOLEAN;

begin
    I := 0;
    while not EOLN(INFILE) and (I < MAX_LINE_WIDTH) do begin
        I := I + 1;
        READ (INFILE, LINE.IMAGE[I]);
    end;
    READLN (INFILE);

    TRAILING_BLANKS := TRUE;
    while TRAILING_BLANKS and (I <> 0) do begin
        if LINE.IMAGE[I] = BLANK then
            I := I - 1
        else
            TRAILING_BLANKS := FALSE
    end;
    LINE.WIDTH := I
end;
```

```
procedure GET_WORD ({from}   var INFILE: TEXT;
                    {giving} var WORD:   LINE_INFO);

{ -- This procedure extracts a word from the input file. }

    var
        I: INTEGER;
        BLANK_CHAR: CHAR;

begin
    while (not EOLN(INFILE)) and (NEXT_CHAR(INFILE) = BLANK) do
        READ (INFILE, BLANK_CHAR);

    I := 0;
    while (not EOLN(INFILE)) and (NEXT_CHAR(INFILE) <> BLANK) do begin
        I := I + 1;
        READ (INFILE, WORD.IMAGE[I])
    end;
    WORD.WIDTH := I
end;


end INPUT_INFO;


{ ------------------------------------------------------- }
```

```
package CONTROL_LINES;
inherit INPUT_INFO;

    const
        MAX_INDENT       = 50;
        MAX_HEADER_WIDTH = 50;
        MAX_NO_SPLIT     = 50;

    type
        COMMAND_NAME = (SINGLESPACE, DOUBLESPACE, HEADER, NEWPAGE,
                        PARAGRAPH,   VERBATIM,    CENTER,
                        INDENT,      NOSPLIT,     ERROR);

        TEXT_STR     = packed array [1..MAX_LINE_WIDTH] of CHAR;

        COMMAND_INFO =
            record
                NAME:        COMMAND_NAME;
                NUMERIC_ARG: INTEGER;
                STRING_ARG:  TEXT_STR;
                STRING_LEN:  INTEGER
            end;

    procedure PARSE_CONTROL_LINE ({using}  LINE: LINE_INFO;
                                  {giving} var CMD: COMMAND_INFO);
end;


{  ------------------------------------------------------ }
```

```
package body CONTROL_LINES;



function DIGIT_VALUE (C: CHAR):  {returns}  INTEGER;
begin
   DIGIT_VALUE := ORD(C) - ORD('0')
end;



function MAKE_UPPER_CASE (C: CHAR): {returns}  CHAR;
{ -- Assumes continuous letter codes. }
begin
   if C in ['a'..'z'] then
      MAKE_UPPER_CASE := CHR(ORD('A') + (ORD(C) - ORD('a')))
   else
      MAKE_UPPER_CASE := C
end;
```

```
procedure PARSE_NUM ({using}  LINE:      LINE_INFO;
                               START_POS: INTEGER;
                    {giving} var CMD:    COMMAND_INFO);

{ -- This procedure analyzes the argument for a NOSPLIT or INDENT command.
  -- If the argument is not a well-formed number, CMD.NAME is set to ERROR.
  -- Otherwise the number is assigned to CMD.ARG. }

    var
        C: CHAR;
        VALUE: INTEGER;
        POSITION: INTEGER;

begin
    VALUE := 0;
    POSITION := START_POS;
    C := LINE.IMAGE[POSITION];

    while (C in ['0'..'9'])
    and (POSITION <= LINE.WIDTH) do begin
        VALUE := 10*VALUE + DIGIT_VALUE(C);
        POSITION := POSITION + 1;
        if POSITION <= LINE.WIDTH then
            C := LINE.IMAGE[POSITION]
    end;

    if POSITION = START_POS then
        begin
            CMD.NAME         := ERROR;
            CMD.NUMERIC_ARG := 0
        end
    else
        CMD.NUMERIC_ARG := VALUE
end;
```

```
procedure PARSE_HEADER ({using}  LINE:       LINE_INFO;
                                 START_POS: INTEGER;
                        {giving} var CMD:    COMMAND_INFO);

{ -- This procedure analyzes the header for a HEADER command. If the
  -- header is invalid, CMD.NAME is set to ERROR. Otherwise the header
  -- is assigned to CMD.STRING_ARG. }

   const
      QUOTE_MARK = '"';
   var
      POSITION: INTEGER;
      LENGTH:   INTEGER;

begin
   if LINE.IMAGE[START_POS] = QUOTE_MARK then begin
      POSITION := START_POS + 1;
      LENGTH := 0;

      while (LINE.IMAGE[POSITION] <> QUOTE_MARK)
      and (POSITION < LINE.WIDTH) do begin
         LENGTH := LENGTH + 1;
         CMD.STRINGARG[LENGTH] := LINE.IMAGE[POSITION];
         POSITION := POSITION + 1
      end;
   end;

   if (LINE.IMAGE[START_POS] <> QUOTE_MARK)
   or (LINE.IMAGE[POSITION]  <> QUOTE_MARK)
   then
      begin
         CMD.NAME := ERROR;
         CMD.STRING_LEN := 0
      end
   else
      CMD.STRING_LEN := LENGTH;
end;
```

```
procedure PARSE_ARG ({using}  LINE:      LINE_INFO;
                               BLANK_POS: INTEGER;
                      {giving} var CMD:   COMMAND_INFO);

{ -- This procedure analyzes the argument for a HEADER, NOSPLIT, or
  -- or INDENT command. If the argument is missing or invalid,
  -- it sets CMD.NAME to ERROR. Otherwise it establishes the
  -- argument for CMD. }

   var
      POSITION: INTEGER;

begin
   POSITION := BLANK_POS;
   while (POSITION <= LINE.WIDTH)
   and (LINE.IMAGE[POSITION] = BLANK) do
        POSITION := POSITION + 1;

   if POSITION > LINE.WIDTH then { -- no arg found }
      CMD.NAME := ERROR
   else if CMD.NAME = HEADER then
      begin
         PARSE_HEADER (LINE, POSITION, CMD);
         if CMD.STRING_LEN > MAX_HEADER_WIDTH then
            CMD.NAME := ERROR
      end
   else if CMD.NAME = NOSPLIT then
      begin
         PARSE_NUM (LINE, POSITION, CMD);
         if CMD.NUMERIC_ARG > MAX_NOSPLIT then
            CMD.NAME := ERROR
      end
   else if CMD.NAME = INDENT then
      begin
         PARSE_NUM (LINE, POSITION, CMD);
         if CMD.NUMERIC_ARG > MAX_INDENT then
            CMD.NAME := ERROR
      end
end;
```

```
procedure PARSE_CONTROL_LINE ({using}  LINE:    LINE_INFO;
                              {giving} var CMD: COMMAND_INFO);

{ -- This procedure analyzes a control line and determines
  -- whether or not it is legal. If it is legal, the command
  -- name and its argument (if any) are established in CMD.
  -- If it is not legal, CMD.NAME is set to ERROR. }

  const
      MAX_NAME_LENGTH = 11;
  type
      CHAR_STRING = packed array[1..MAX_NAME_LENGTH] of CHAR;
  var
      BLANK_FOUND: BOOLEAN;
      BLANK_POS:   INTEGER;
      I, POSITION: INTEGER;
      NAME_STR:    CHAR_STRING;

begin
  BLANK_FOUND := FALSE;
  for I := 1 to MAX_NAME_LENGTH do begin
      POSITION := I + 1;  { -- skip over control char }
      if (POSITION > LINE.WIDTH) or BLANK_FOUND then
          NAME_STR[I] := BLANK
      else if LINE.IMAGE[POSITION] = BLANK then
          begin
              NAME_STR[I] := BLANK;
              BLANK_FOUND := TRUE;
              BLANK_POS   := POSITION
          end
      else
          NAME_STR[I] := MAKE_UPPER_CASE(LINE.IMAGE[POSITION])
  end;

  if NAME_STR = 'SINGLESPACE' then
      CMD.NAME := SINGLESPACE
  else if NAME_STR = 'DOUBLESPACE' then
      CMD.NAME := DOUBLESPACE
  else if NAME_STR = 'PARAGRAPH  ' then
      CMD.NAME := PARAGRAPH
  else if NAME_STR = 'VERBATIM   ' then
      CMD.NAME := VERBATIM
  else if NAME_STR = 'CENTER     ' then
      CMD.NAME := CENTER
```

```
   else if NAME_STR = 'NEWPAGE     ' then
      CMD.NAME := NEWPAGE
   else if NAME_STR = 'HEADER      ' then
      CMD.NAME := HEADER
   else if NAME_STR = 'INDENT      ' then
      CMD.NAME := INDENT
   else if NAME_STR = 'NOSPLIT     ' then
      CMD.NAME := NOSPLIT
   else
      CMD.NAME := ERROR;

   if CMD.NAME in [HEADER, NOSPLIT, INDENT] then
      PARSE_ARG (LINE, BLANK_POS, CMD)
end;


end CONTROL_LINES;

{ -------------------------------------------------------- }
```

```
package PAGE_LAYOUT;

   const
      { -- Vertical }
      LINES_PER_PAGE = 66;
      TOP_MARGIN     = 8;
      BOTTOM_MARGIN  = 8;
      PAGE_NUM_LINE  = 6;

      { -- Horizontal }
      CHARS_PER_LINE   = 85;
      LEFT_MARGIN      = 12;
      RIGHT_MARGIN     = 10;
      TEXT_WIDTH       = 63;    { CHARS_PER_LINE - LEFT_MARGIN - RIGHT_MARGIN }
      MAX_TEXT_WIDTH   = 73;    { CHARS_PER_LINE - LEFT_MARGIN }
      PARA_INDENT      = 5;
      MAX_BUFFER_WIDTH = 170;   { A challenge }

   type
      SINGLE_OR_DOUBLE = (SINGLE, DOUBLE);

      TEXT_IMAGE = packed array[1..MAX_BUFFER_WIDTH] of CHAR;
      TEXT_INFO  =
         record
            WIDTH: 0..MAX_BUFFER_WIDTH;
            IMAGE: TEXT_IMAGE
         end;

      HEADER_STR  = packed array[1..MAX_TEXT_WIDTH] of CHAR;
      HEADER_INFO =
         record
            WIDTH: 0..MAX_TEXT_WIDTH;
            IMAGE: HEADER_STR
         end;

      PAGE_INFO =
         record
            LINE_NUM: INTEGER;
            PAGE_NUM: INTEGER;
            HEADER:   HEADER_INFO;
            SPACING:  SINGLE_OR_DOUBLE
         end;
```

```
   procedure START_DOCUMENT  (var OUTFILE: TEXT; var PAGE: PAGE_INFO);
   procedure FINISH_DOCUMENT (var OUTFILE: TEXT; var PAGE: PAGE_INFO);

   procedure NEXT_PAGE        (var OUTFILE: TEXT; var PAGE: PAGE_INFO);
   procedure NEXT_LINE        (var OUTFILE: TEXT; var PAGE: PAGE_INFO);

   procedure PRINT_TEXT_LINE (var BUFFER: TEXT_INFO;
                                 var OUTFILE: TEXT; var PAGE: PAGE_INFO);
   procedure PRINT_ERROR_LINE (LINE: LINE_INFO;
                                  var OUTFILE: TEXT; var PAGE: PAGE_INFO);

   procedure SET_HEADER      (VALUE: TEXT_STR; LENGTH: INTEGER;
                                var PAGE: PAGE_INFO);

   procedure SET_NO_SPLIT (NUM_LINES: INTEGER;
                                 var OUTFILE: TEXT; var PAGE: PAGE_INFO);

   procedure SET_SPACING  (OPTION: SINGLE_OR_DOUBLE;
                                var PAGE: PAGE_INFO);


end;


{ -------------------------------------------------------- }


package body PAGE_LAYOUT;

   const
      START_PRINT_COL = 13;  { -- LEFT_MARGIN + 1 }
      END_PRINT_COL   = 75;  { -- CHARS_PER_LINE - RIGHT_MARGIN }

      FIRST_TEXT_LINE =  9;  { -- TOP_MARGIN + 1 }
      LAST_TEXT_LINE  = 58;  { -- LINES_PER_PAGE - BOTTOM_MARGIN }

      BLANK = ' ';
      NORMAL_MARGIN = '              ';
      ERROR_MARGIN  = '**            ';
```

```
procedure START_DOCUMENT (var OUTFILE: TEXT;
                          var PAGE:   PAGE_INFO);

{ -- This procedure establishes the protocols for the first page of output. }

    var
      I: INTEGER;

begin
    for I := 1 to (FIRST_TEXT_LINE - 1) do
      WRITELN (OUTFILE);

    PAGE.PAGE_NUM := 1;
    PAGE.LINE_NUM := FIRST_TEXT_LINE;

    for I := 1 to MAX_HEADER_WIDTH do
      PAGE.HEADER.IMAGE[I] := BLANK;
    PAGE.HEADER.WIDTH := 0;

    PAGE.SPACING := SINGLE
end;




procedure FINISH_DOCUMENT ({updating} var OUTFILE: TEXT;
                                      var PAGE:   PAGE_INFO);

{ -- This procedure completes the last page of a document. If no lines have
  -- been printed (an empty INFILE), a message is printed. }

    var
      I, NUM_BLANK_LINES: INTEGER;

begin
    if (PAGE.PAGE_NUM = 1) and (PAGE.LINE_NUM = FIRST_TEXT_LINE) then
      WRITE (OUTFILE, '** NO TEXT GIVEN AS INPUT.');

    NUM_BLANK_LINES := LINES_PER_PAGE - PAGE.LINE_NUM + 1;
    for I := 1 to NUM_BLANK_LINES do
      WRITELN (OUTFILE)
end;
```

```
procedure NEXT_PAGE (({updating} var OUTFILE: TEXT;
                                   var PAGE:    PAGE_INFO);

{ -- This procedure completes the current page and starts a new one,
  -- including a new page number and page header. }

    var
        I, NUM_BLANK_LINES: INTEGER;

begin
    NUM_BLANK_LINES := LINES_PER_PAGE - PAGE.LINE_NUM;
    for I := 1 to NUM_BLANK_LINES do
        WRITELN (OUTFILE);

    PAGE.PAGE_NUM := PAGE.PAGE_NUM + 1;
    for I := 1 to (PAGE_NUM_LINE - 1) do
        WRITELN (OUTFILE);

    WRITE (OUTFILE, NORMAL_MARGIN);
    WRITE (OUTFILE, PAGE.PAGE_NUM : 1);
    WRITE (OUTFILE, BLANK, BLANK);
    for I := 1 to PAGE.HEADER.WIDTH do
        WRITE (OUTFILE, PAGE.HEADER.IMAGE[I]);

    for I := PAGE_NUM_LINE to FIRST_TEXT_LINE do
        WRITELN(OUTFILE);
    PAGE.LINE_NUM := FIRST_TEXT_LINE
end;
```

```
procedure NEXT_LINE ({updating} var OUTFILE: TEXT;
                                 var PAGE:    PAGE_INFO);

{ -- This procedure causes an advance to a new line. }

begin
   if PAGE.LINE_NUM = LAST_TEXT_LINE then
      NEXT_PAGE (OUTFILE, PAGE)
   else
      begin
         WRITELN (OUTFILE);
         PAGE.LINE_NUM := PAGE.LINE_NUM + 1
      end;

   if PAGE.SPACING = DOUBLE then
      if PAGE.LINE_NUM = LAST_TEXT_LINE then
         NEXT_PAGE (OUTFILE, PAGE)
      else
         begin
            WRITELN (OUTFILE);
            PAGE.LINE_NUM := PAGE.LINE_NUM + 1
         end
end;
```

```
procedure PRINT_TEXT_LINE ({updating} var BUFFER:  TEXT_INFO;
                                       var OUTFILE: TEXT;
                                       var PAGE:    PAGE_INFO);

{ -- This procedure outputs a line of text for printing. If the line is
  -- too long, excess characters are printed in the right margin and
  -- continued on the following line, with no indent. }

   var
      I: INTEGER;

begin
   WRITE (OUTFILE, NORMAL_MARGIN);
   if BUFFER.WIDTH <= MAX_TEXT_WIDTH then
      for I := 1 to BUFFER.WIDTH do
         WRITE (OUTFILE, BUFFER.IMAGE[I])
   else
      begin
        for I := 1 to MAX_TEXT_WIDTH do
           WRITE (OUTFILE, BUFFER.IMAGE[I]);
        NEXT_LINE (OUTFILE, PAGE);
        WRITE (OUTFILE, NORMAL_MARGIN);
        for I := MAX_TEXT_WIDTH + 1 to BUFFER.WIDTH do
           WRITE (OUTFILE, BUFFER.IMAGE[I])
      end;

   NEXT_LINE (OUTFILE, PAGE);
   BUFFER.WIDTH := 0
end;
```

```
procedure PRINT_ERROR_LINE ({using}    LINE: LINE_INFO;
                            {updating} var OUTFILE: TEXT;
                            var PAGE: PAGE_INFO);

{ -- This procedure outputs an erroneous control line. }

    var
        I: INTEGER;

begin
    WRITE (OUTFILE, ERROR_MARGIN);
    if LINE.WIDTH <= MAX_TEXT_WIDTH then
        for I := 1 to LINE.WIDTH do
            WRITE (OUTFILE, LINE.IMAGE[I])
    else
        begin
        for I := 1 to MAX_TEXT_WIDTH do
            WRITE (OUTFILE, LINE.IMAGE[I]);
        NEXT_LINE (OUTFILE, PAGE);
        WRITE (OUTFILE, NORMAL_MARGIN);
        for I := MAX_TEXT_WIDTH + 1 to LINE.WIDTH do
            WRITE (OUTFILE, LINE.IMAGE[I])
        end;
    NEXT_LINE (OUTFILE, PAGE)
end;
```

```
procedure SET_HEADER ({using} VALUE:   TEXT_STR;
                                LENGTH: INTEGER;
                       {updating} var PAGE: PAGE_INFO);

{ -- Establishes a new header for subsequent pages. }

   var
      I: INTEGER;

begin
   for I := 1 to LENGTH do
      PAGE.HEADER.IMAGE[I] := VALUE[I];
   PAGE.HEADER.WIDTH := LENGTH
end;




procedure SET_NOSPLIT ({using} NUM_LINES: INTEGER;
                        {updating} var INFILE: TEXT;
                                    var PAGE: PAGE_INFO);

{ -- This procedure checks that there are NUM_LINES remaining
  -- on the current page. If not, a new page is established. }

   var
      BLOCK_SIZE: INTEGER;

begin
   if (PAGE.SPACING = SINGLE) then
      BLOCK_SIZE := NUM_LINES
   else { -- DOUBLE spacing }
      BLOCK_SIZE := 2*NUM_LINES - 1;
   if (PAGE.LINE_NUM + BLOCK_SIZE - 1) > LAST_TEXT_LINE then
      NEXT_PAGE (OUTFILE, PAGE)
end;
```

```
procedure SET_SPACING ({using} OPTION: SINGLE_OR_DOUBLE;
                       {updating} var PAGE: PAGE_INFO);

{ -- Sets indicator for SINGLE or DOUBLE spacing. }

begin
   PAGE.SPACING := OPTION
end;


end PAGE_LAYOUT;

{ ------------------------------------------------- }
```

References

[Ada Rationale, 1979]
Rationale for the Design of the Green Programming Language, Honeywell, Inc. and Cii Honeywell Bull, March, 1979

[Alsys, 1986]
Alsys PC At Ada Compiler User's Guide, Alsys, Inc., Waltham, Mass., 1986

[Brooks, 1975]
Frederick P. Brooks
The Mythical Man-Month, Addison-Wesley, Reading, Mass., 1975

[Cave and Maymon, 1984]
William C. Cave and Gilbert W. Maymon, *Software Lifecycle Management,* Macmillan Publishing Co., New York, 1984

[Curtis, 1981]
Bill Curtis, Editor
Human Factors in Software Development, IEEE Computer Society, Box 80452, Los Angeles, Calif. 90080, 1981

[Dickson et al., 1986]
Gary Dickson, Geraldine DeSanctis, and D. J. McBride, "Understanding the Effectiveness of Computer Graphics for Decision Support," *Communications of the ACM,* January, 1986

[Fairley, 1985]
Richard Fairley
Software Engineering Concepts, McGraw-Hill, New York, 1985

[Good et al., 1984]
Michael Good, John Whiteside, Dennis Wixon, and Sandy Jones, "Building a User-Derived Interface," *Communications of the ACM,* October, 1984

[Gould et al., 1987]
John Gould, Stephen Bois, Stephen Levy, John Richards, and Jim Schoonard, "The 1984 Olympic Message System," (To appear in) *Communications of the ACM,* 1987

[Hoare, 1981]
C.A.R. Hoare, "The Emperor's Old Clothes," *Communications of the ACM,* February, 1981

[Jensen and Wirth, 1974]
Kathleen Jensen and Niklaus Wirth, *Pascal User Manual and Report,* Third Edition, Springer-Verlag, New York, 1974

[Ledgard, 1986]
Henry Ledgard, guest editor, Special Section on Human Aspects of Computing, *Communications of the ACM,* July, 1986

[Levy, 1985]
Leon S. Levy, *Software Economics* (in preparation), AT&T Bell Labs, Whippany, N.J., 1985

[Levy, 1985]
Leon S. Levy, "Metaprogramming Method and Its Economic Justification," (informal manuscript) AT&T Bell Labs, Whippany, N.J., 1985

[Macro and Buxton, 1987]
Allen Macro and John Buxton, *The Craft of Software Engineering,* Addison-Wesley, Wokingham, Berks, England, 1987

[Rubenstein and Hersh, 1984]
Richard Rubenstein and Harry Hersh, *The Human Factor,* Digital Press, Burlington Mass., 1984

[Rushinek and Rushinek, 1986]
Avi Rushinek and Sara F. Rushinek, "What Makes Users Happy," *Communications of the ACM,* July, 1986

[Singer et al., 1980]
Andrew Singer, Henry Ledgard, and Jon Hueras, "The Annotated Assistant: A Step Towards Human Engineering," *IEEE Transactions on Software Engineering SE-7, no. 4,* 1980

[Sommerville, 1985]
Ian Sommerville, *Software Engineering,* 2d ed., Addison-Wesley, Reading, Mass., 1985

[Vessey and Weber, 1986]
Iris Vessey and Ron Weber, "Structured Tools and Conditional Logic: An Empirical Investigation," *Communications of the ACM,* January, 1986

[Weinberg, 1986]
Gerald M. Weinberg, *Becoming a Technical Leader,* Dorset House, New York, 1986

[Weinberg, 1971]
Gerald M. Weinberg, *The Psychology of Computer Programming,* Van Nostrand Reinhold, New York, 1971

[Yourdon, 1979]
Edward Yourdon, *Managing the Structured Techniques,* Prentice-Hall, Englewood Cliffs N.J., 1979

Index

abbreviation 75, 99, 145
  first-letter 95-99
Ada® 102, 106
aficionado 1, 6
Algol 60 15
algorithm 16, 21
amateur 1-5, 6, 9, 10, 63
  Charlie 71-74, 85
archives 44, 65
array 16
audit 26-29, 37-39

benchmarks 9, 22-25, 26, 34-36,
  39, 91
bickering 57, 58
boasting 57
bright star 60-61
Brooks, Frederick 47, 129

C 106
Cave, William 16
Charlie 71-74, 85
chief programmer 44-45, 47
coding 24-29
  top-down 20, 21
  standards 21, 22, 24

collective ego 43, 61, 66
command 76-78, 79-80, 81, 99,
  150-157, 163-165
comments 16, 61-62, 66
  header 159-160
commercial product 132-133, 134
complaining 57
complexity 74-75, 88
construction 17, 20, 21
contract software 17, 131-132, 134
correctness 4
crew 41-43, 49, 52-53
  combat 41, 52
  gaggle 41-42, 52
  exulation 41-42, 52
cursor movement 82-84
Curtis, William 112

declarations 102
data gathering 111
decomposition 104-108, 171-175
definition 19, 21
design notation 104-106
Delta Soft Products 26-27, 37-39
design 11, 16, 19, 21, 28, 38, 71-85,
  87-99

control-line based   169-170
line-by-line   168-169
mode-based   168, 170
notation   106
program   167-171
prompting symbol   80
development   16-17, 67
documentation   5, 9-10, 19, 21-23,
   26, 34, 37, 48, 65, 80-81, 88-90,
   134-135
domination   57, 58
dynamic debugging tools   71

ego   43, 56, 61, 66
collective   43, 61, 66
individual   43, 61
egoless   61-63, 66, 131
misconception   62
empirical methods   111-127
erroneous input   16
experiment   111-127
data gathering   111
design notation   120-121
naming   116-117
procedures   117-120
program layout   112-116
exulation   41-42, 52

facade   32, 90
Fairley, Richard   22, 33
feedback   22-29, 33, 62
formal specification   19, 21, 26-29
Fortran   15
fragmentation   48
functional specification   9, 19, 35-36,
   37, 52, 158-165, 173

gaggle   41-42, 52
Gannon, John   102
global variables   101
Good, Michael   74, 99
Gould, John   134

header comments   159-160
hierarchical team   47

hobbyist   4
humility   58
human engineering   72, 73, 75-76, 79-85,
   144
human factors   33, 56, 73, 74-75, 87-99
misconceptions   71-85, 111-127

immobile   7
implementation   10, 34
facade   32
individual ego   43, 61
inherit clause   104
input   4, 10, 95, 103, 161
erroneous   16
installation   22

journeyman   7

keywords   79-80, 98

layout   112-116, 139-177
Ledgard, Henry   99, 112
Levy, Leon   33
line-by-line design   168-169

Macro, Allen   22
Mayer, Richard   120, 121
maintenance   11
management   60, 62-63, 69, 132-133
screen   83-84
menus   76-80, 81, 95-99
meta-programming   33
Mills, Harlan   47
misconceptions   62
human factors   71-85
mode-based design   168-170
Modula-2   102, 106

negativism   57
notation   106
naming   116-117 novice   2, 6

organization   46, 49, 50-52
output   4, 10, 20, 148, 161
layout   16, 146

packages 101-108, 171-173
  bodies 102-104
  declarations 102
  design notation 104-106
  sorting 5
  visible part 104-106

personality 56-63
  bickering 57, 58
  boasting 57
  complaining 57
  domination 57, 58
  humility 58
  negativism 57
  singling out 57, 58
  talent overload 56, 57

procedure 102-104, 107-108, 112,
    117-120
  implementation part 103
  visible part 103

professional 1-3, 6-12, 58, 63
  programming 43, 65
  software 10

program 16, 139-209
  construction 17
  correctness 4
  decomposition 104-108, 171-175
  design 16
  development 16-17
  layout 112-116, 139-177
  maintenance 11
  readability 4, 9
  specification 16
  testing 4, 11, 17
  text-editing 10
  text-formatting 139-140, 171-209

programmers 1-12, 50-52, 58-63
  amateur 1-5, 6, 9, 10, 12, 63
  chief 44-45
  immobile 7
  novice 2, 6

population 8
professional 1-3, 6-12, 58, 63
  P-sub-A 6, 9, 12

programming 2, 43, 61-63
  ego 43
  egoless 61-63
  group 43
  personality 55
  practice 34, 39
  procedure 55
  process 55
  team 10-11, 41-53, 55

programming group 43, 61
  stress 61, 81

project 55, 61-63, 129
  commercial product 132-133, 134
  contract software 131-132, 134
  definition 19, 21
  ideal 135
  plan 26-29
  team 43, 50-52
  university 130-131, 134

project definition 19, 21
project plan 26-29

prototypes 15, 19, 21, 29, 31-39,
    88, 90-92, 130
  tool building 33

P-sub-A 6, 9, 12
quality 12, 28, 33, 53, 89
quasar 60-61

random permutation 16
requirements, user 5, 9, 17, 23,
    146, 173
routine 44, 103
  control 171
  I/O 48, 171
  random number 16
  utility 16, 107, 171

screen layout 83-84, 108
screen management 83-84
Singer, Andrew 96, 99
stress 61, 81
    muscle 83
software 4, 11, 33-34, 44-47, 52-53,
    91-93
    contract 17, 131-132, 134
    decomposition 101-108
    development 17, 67
    engineering 15
    interactive 93-97
    professional 10
    successful 129-135
software lifecycle 3, 5, 9, 15-29,
    31-32, 34-39, 63, 82, 88, 130,
    133-134
    construction 20, 21
    design 21
    feedback 22-29, 33, 62
    installation 22
    formal specification 19, 21, 26-29
    functional specification 9, 19, 35-3
        37, 52, 158-165, 173
    project definition 19, 21
    prototypes 15, 19, 21, 29, 31-39,
        88, 90-92, 130
    text-book 19-22
specification
    formal 19, 21, 26-29
    functional 9, 19, 35-36
    program 16
    user 134-135, 140-146, 158, 160
Spread-Calc 26-29, 37-39
Spread-Calc II 37, 38
sorting 5
standards 21, 22, 34
subprogram 101-102
subsets 80-81
system mentality 9
syntax 76, 95-99
    notational 76
    packages 103
    prose-like 76

talent overload 56, 57
team 10, 41-53, 55, 56-63, 104-126
    chief programmer 44-45, 47
    democratic 44
    fragmentation 48
    hierarchical 47
    leader-based 44, 47
    management 60, 62-63, 69
    organization 46, 49, 50-52
    problems 59, 60
    professional programming 43, 65
    solutions 60
    surgical 47
    walkthroughs 67-69
testing 4, 11, 17, 20, 21, 53
    user 19, 21, 29, 32-33, 87, 90-93,
        112, 126
tool building 33
transfer user 74

user friendly 72
user manual 9, 10, 19, 21, 24, 71, 88-90,
    146-157, 158, 173
user requirements 5, 9, 17, 23, 146, 173
user specification 134-135, 140-146,
    158-160

visible part 103, 104-106
Vessey, Iris 121

walkthroughs 43, 53, 65-69
    meeting 68-69
    review 69
Weber, San 29, 36
Weinberg, Gerald 44, 56
Wirth, Niklaus 102
work reading 9, 43, 52, 65-69

ABOUT THE AUTHOR

HENRY LEDGARD received his B.A. from Tufts University and his Ph.D. from the Massachusetts Institute of Technology in 1969.

After a post-graduate year at Oxford, he joined the faculty of Johns Hopkins University where he was influenced by the design ideas of Harlan Mills. Concentrating on projects involving measuring program complexity, he came to believe that broader approaches based on the human comprehension of programs hold the key.

After two years at Johns Hopkins, he joined the faculty at the University of Massachusetts. Mainly through his work with Andrew Singer, he developed theories and ideas for the practice of software human engineering—that is, the human user seems to have been disregarded in the drive for more powerful systems.

In 1977, Dr. Ledgard participated in the Ada project, the design of a new programming language. The project itself was noteworthy in that not only were such issues as the role of program modules and the potential of separate compilation discussed, but seemingly innocuous issues such as the appropriate use or non-use of comments and program layout were considered with a positive emphasis toward more professional programming.

In 1983 and 1984, Dr. Ledgard served as tutor in several seminars offered as the "Senior Software Engineering Course" sponsored by Philips Electronics. The students were professional software engineers with varying degrees of experience, released from their duties for seven weeks to devote their full efforts to this seminar. Formal topics included the role of a functional specification, design notations, and the resolution of conflicts within a programming team. Free discussion periods emphasized working habits of programmers, naming in programs, and how schedules affect the quality of a project.

In addition to the Philips project, in recent years Dr. Ledgard has been a consultant to Digital Electronics Corporation and Alsys, Inc. In 1979, he established his own consulting, seminar, and writing practice. Among his books are an early monograph on human factors, the *Programming Proverbs* series, *Ada: An Introduction, Elementary Basic and Elementary Pascal,* co-authored with Andrew Singer, and *Programming Language Landscape,* co-authored with Michael Marcotty. His latest works are *Professional Pascal, Pascal With Excellence* (with John Tauer), and *C With Excellence* (in preparation).

Dr. Ledgard's professional areas are software engineering, human factors, and programming languages. He resides with his family on Drummer Hill Road, RFD 3, Amherst, Massachusetts.